Lauren Quin

Eyelets of Alkaline

January 31 – March 28, 2026

1201 South La Brea Avenue
Los Angeles

PACE

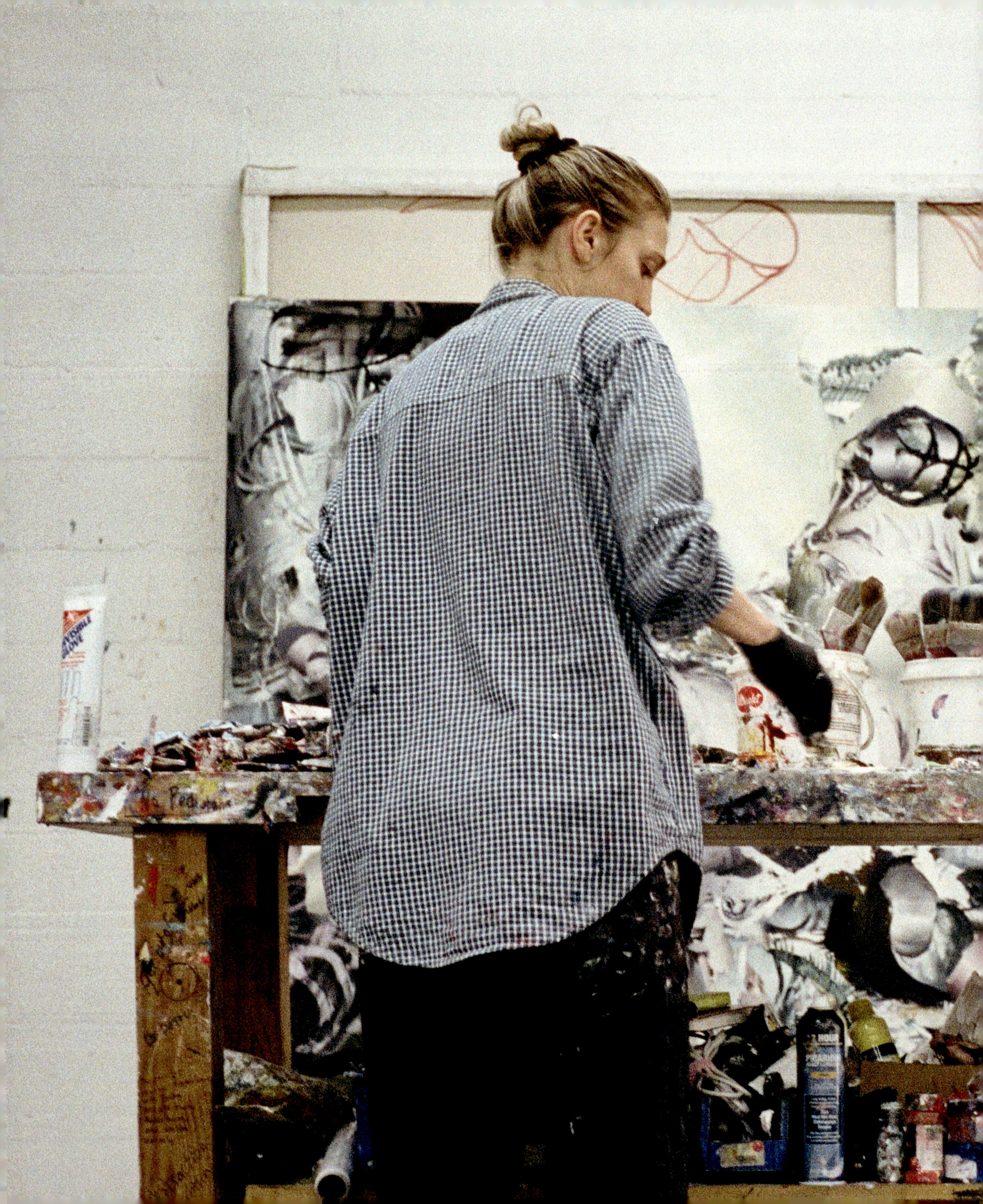

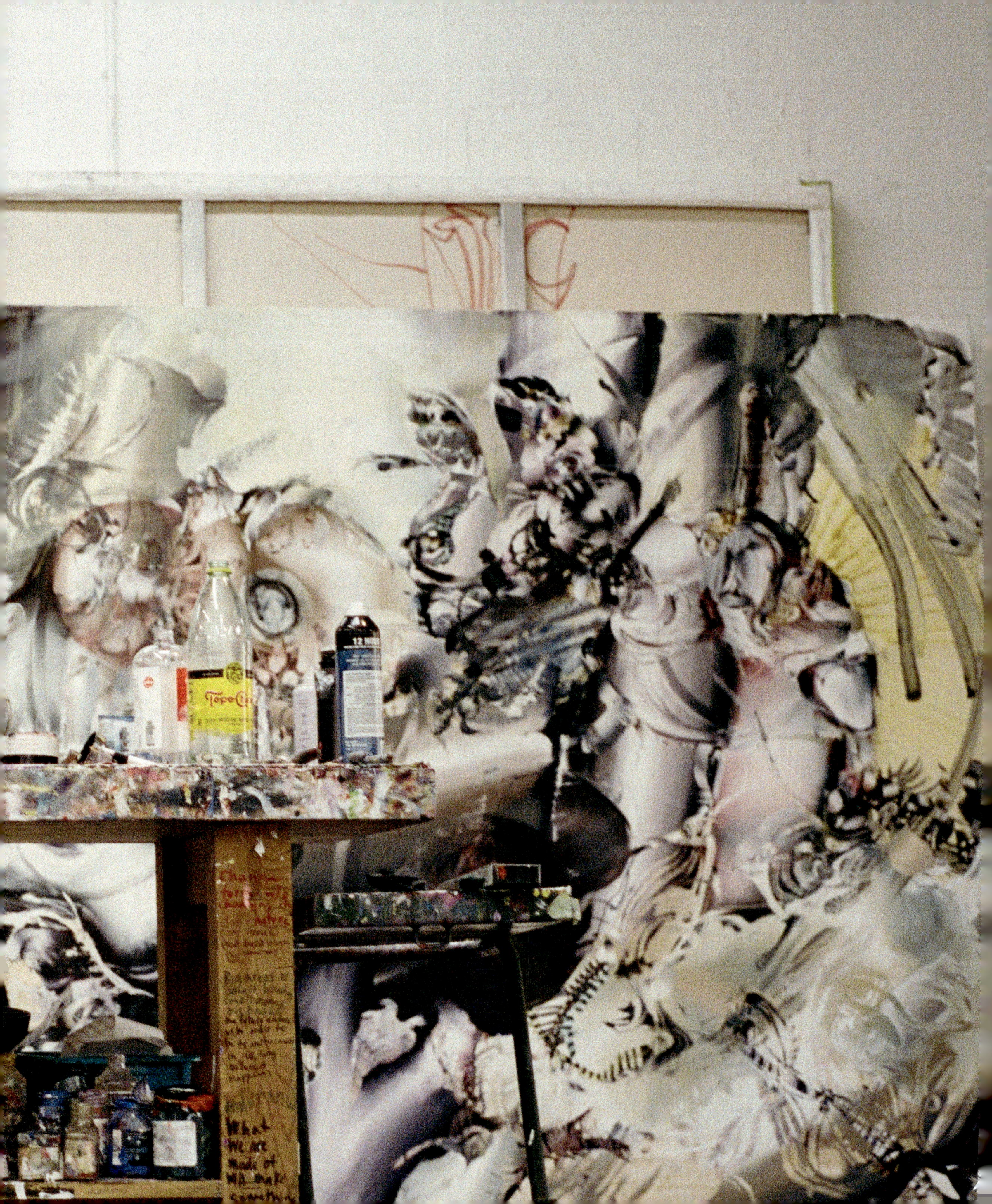

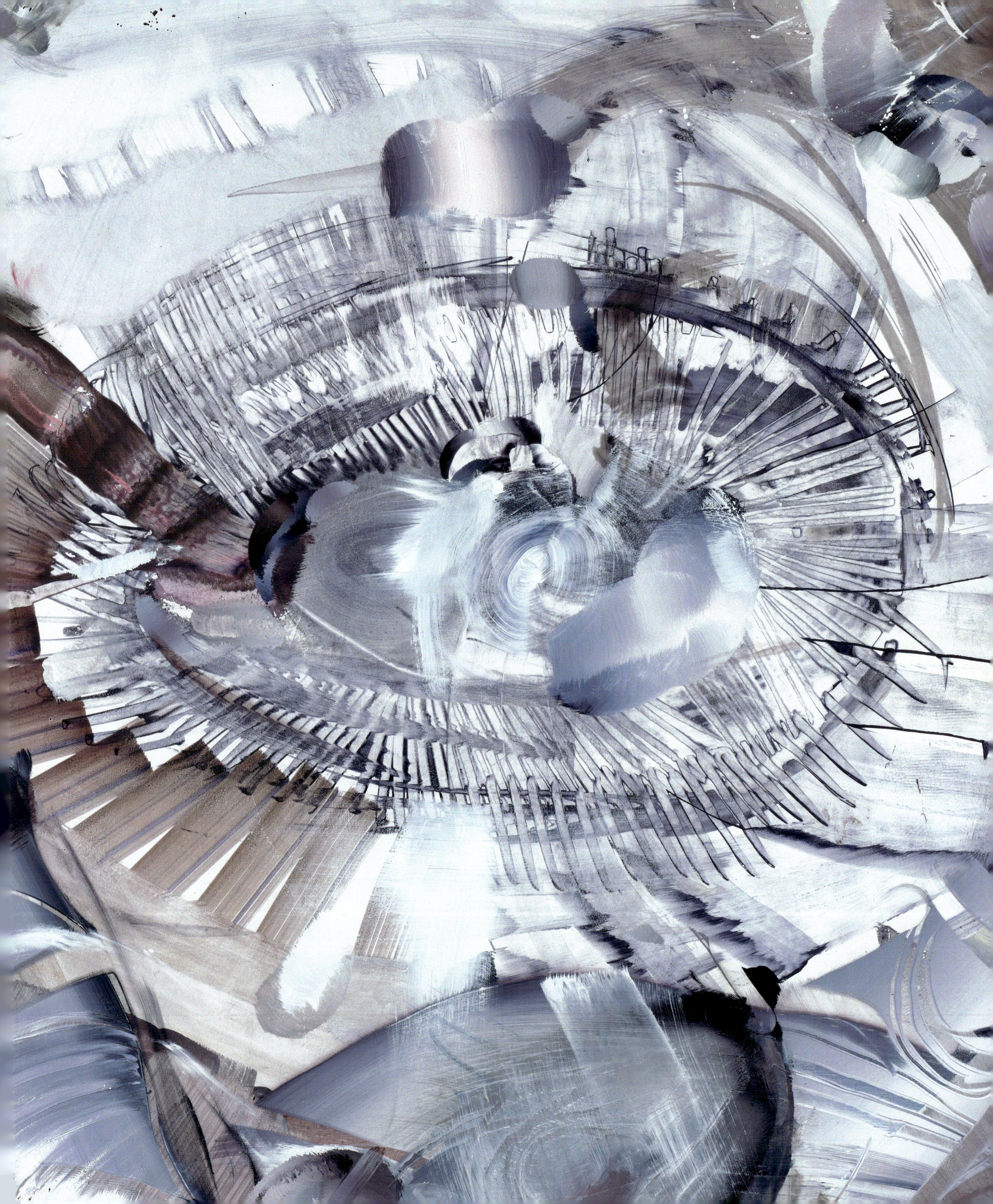

Motion Implied in the Surface of the Bird

Ariana Reines

"What it means to draw a hole... you can't draw a hole. It just looks like a sunburst... or a spider."

In Lauren's studio yesterday I noticed one of her paintings pulling—physically pulling on my right eye. I turned toward another, and it exerted such a strong suctioning effect on both my eyeballs we had to step aside from it to keep talking.

Maybe it was my eyes adjusting to surfaces that simultaneously imply depth and burst out toward me, or maybe it was an effect of transfigured motion.

Transfigured motion... what do I mean.

I mean that the viewer can *feel* the movement of the paintings' making, without needing to know anything formal about painting as such—its history, its discourses. You feel the energy of depth and explosion, you feel an intensity of time layered, you feel color, you sense ambiguity and depth.

These are sensations, not ideas.

I have been thinking about the velocity of understanding, a sense that these artworks may be "about" being in motion: they evoke their own afterimage before you even turn away. Any mind will sense rhyme—will conjure forms and textures from memory to make sense of what it sees—but that is only the beginning of finding out what the paintings really mean and do.

You delve into your own past; you conjure, dredge up fragments of long-submerged experience to justify why what you might describe as a jagged crown upon the sun (for example) feels uncannily familiar: feasting upon abstraction, the soul starts to fabricate rhyme.

An algorithm works to conjure—even parody—your future by making calculations based on what has attracted, what has held your attention in the past. It is a math against anomaly, a foreclosure of the future.

Abstraction is not an algorithm, a painting is not a math, a painting takes place right now, and it changes you right now.

This is only the beginning. In letting go of your own conjurings and associations, a dizziness comes. A surface that had seemed to draw you into its complex depths suddenly bursts out toward you.

The sensation of being plunged into a torrent of stars.

The feeling—and almost fragrance—of grasses, leaves, small secretive animals, and bugs and birds at night, of more creatures than you can possibly see—but you sense them—you feel them in motion, absolutely in motion, real motion causing a disturbance in the air.

The hue of coagulated blood elaborating a realm sobered of color, but color keeps proving it's more than it seems.

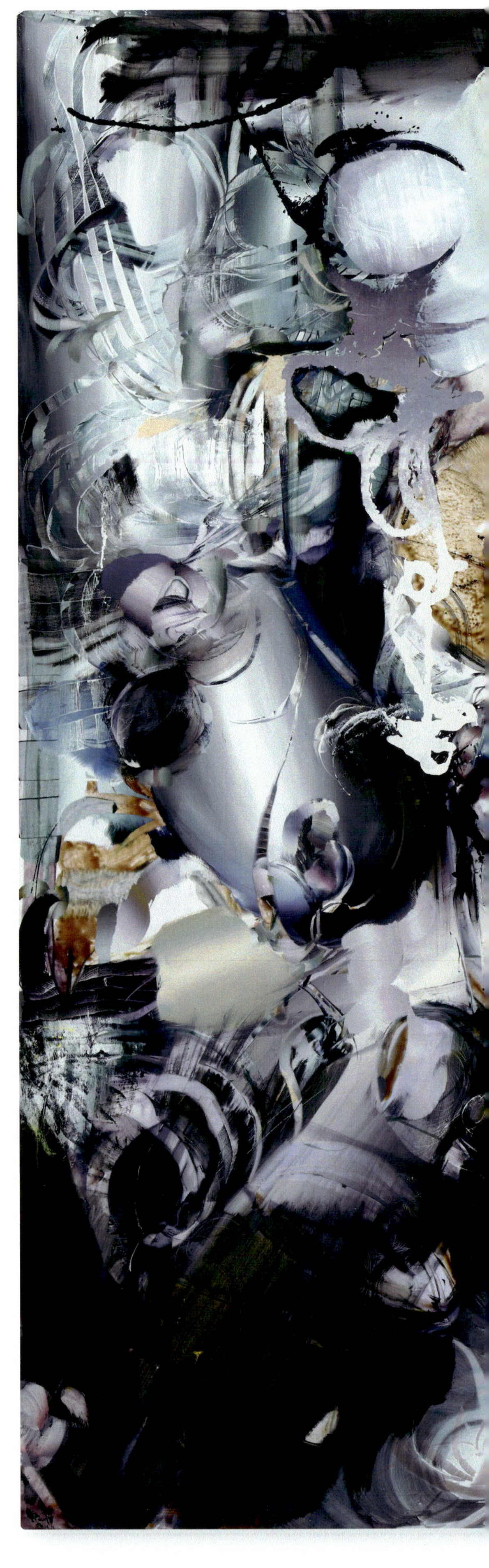

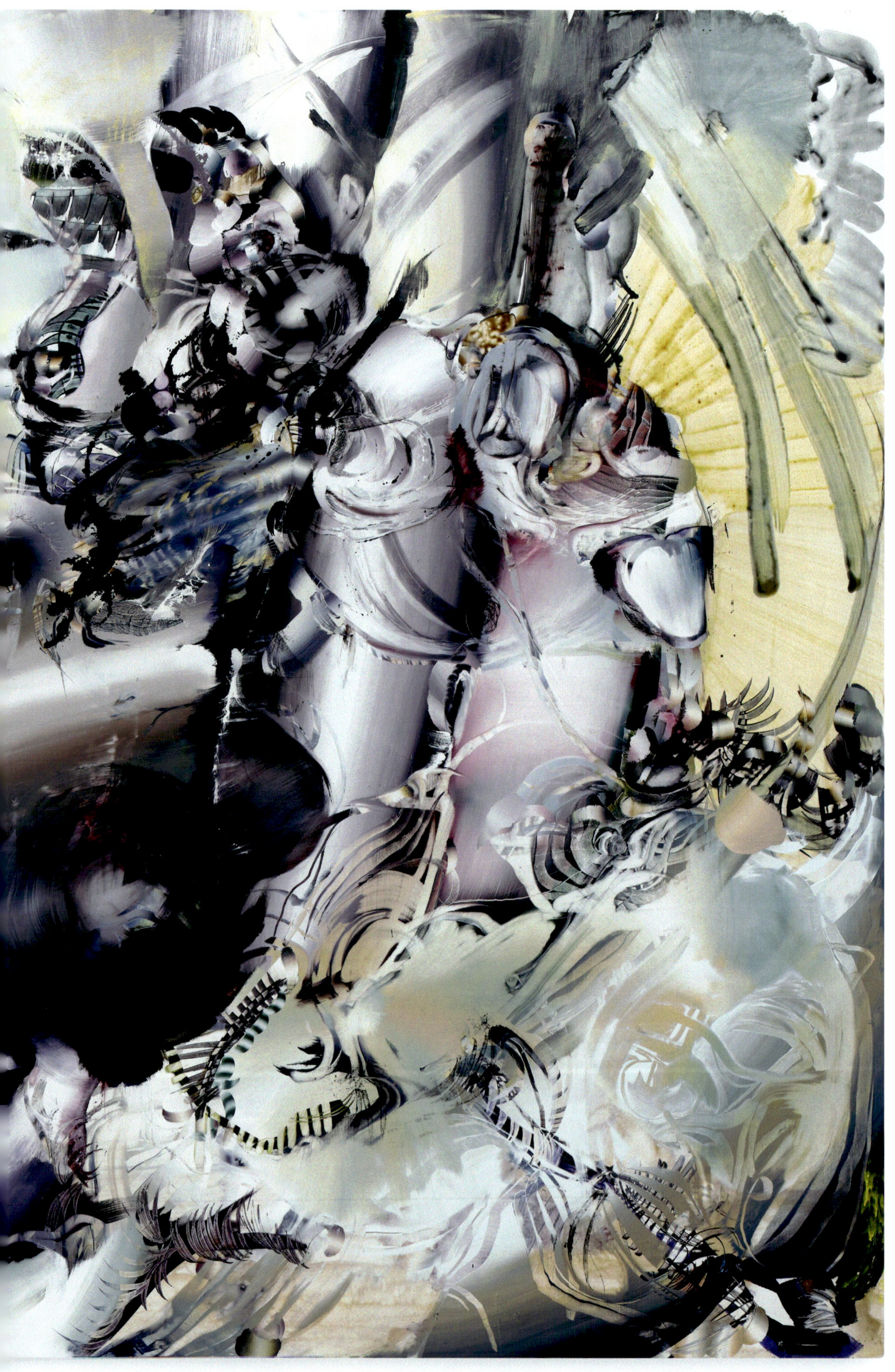

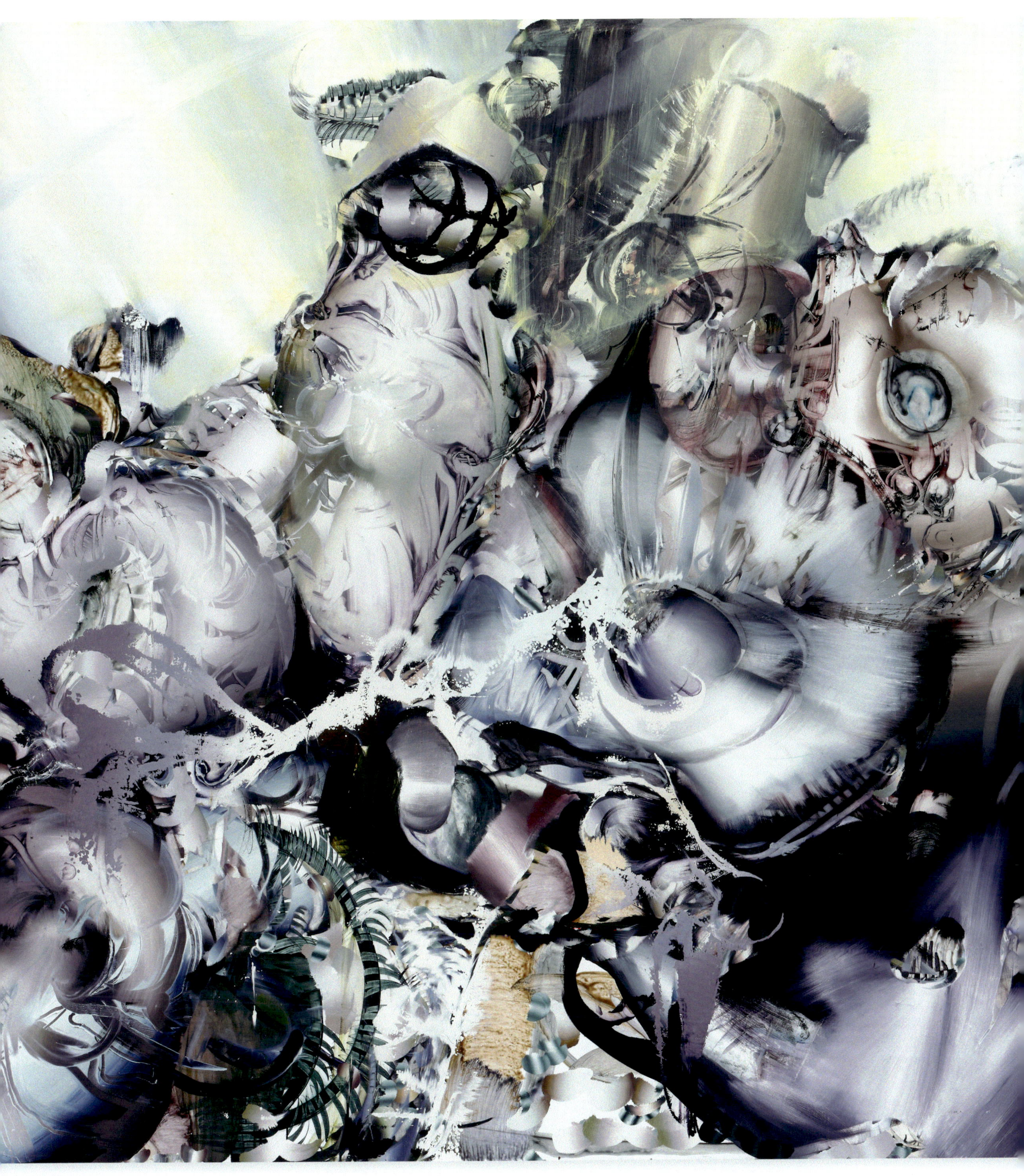

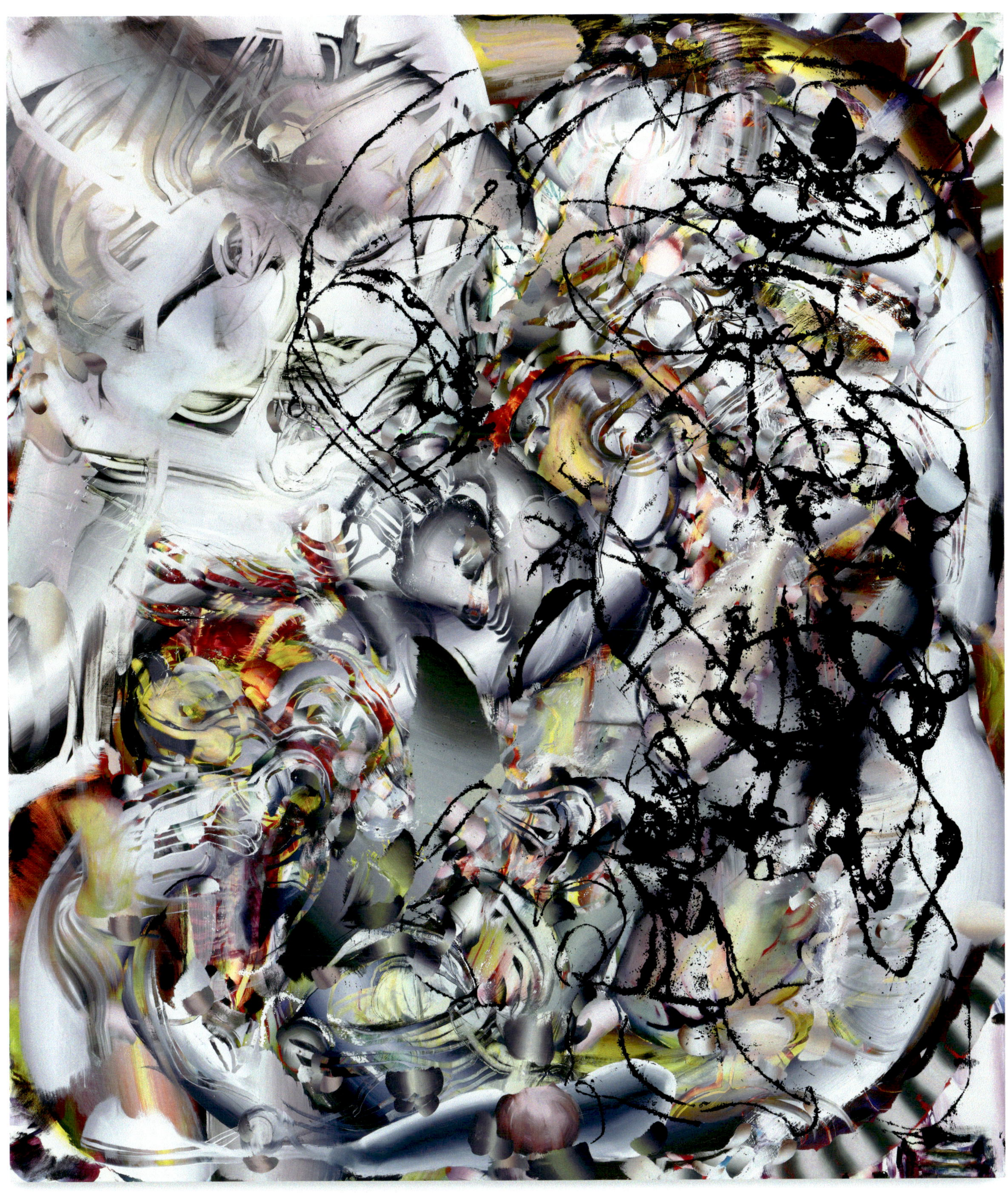

"Are you comfortable with the term abstraction?" I asked. "I take the tradition seriously," Lauren said, "and I want to be good to it."

I found myself thinking about painting's relationship to dance—like there's a difference between literally painting dancers (Degas, Matisse, Silke Otto-Knapp) and *being* dance—wait a minute. I think what I mean is no, I was wrong just now—there's no difference between dance and painting, between the painting of a dancer and the movement of the painter, no real difference that I can perceive.

"How can we know the dancer from the dance?" asked Yeats. But—

I seem to be discovering that I don't need to know. That I don't care.

The dancer is the dance… the dance is the dancer… no?

To settle this another way, for myself at least: dance is a branch of painting, or painting is a form of dance.

As night fell while we talked in Lauren's studio, a former plant nursery partly open to a courtyard, where rats would soon commence their squeaking through the palms—

it occurred to me that it could be a *fact* (after all, I experienced it literally) that in moving toward you *and* recoiling, all at once—in seeming to leap out at you while also elaborating an abyss, whoops of energy starred by leaves, claws, eggs, and eyes—an intensity this layered of involution and outburst *has* to affect, to physically affect and *move* the air that touches its surface.

Like singing into a whirring fan—did you ever do that when you were little?—find yourself entranced by the feeling and the sound of your own voice chopped up by the severed air…?

As if the surface of a painting could beat the air like egg whites, beat the air like a bird's wings do, or cut through it like a dancer.

—and I think that we feel—I know that *I* feel—the painter's body moving even now, and that this historical movement, historical because it made the mark that I see, has been layered into time, into deep time, and so it stays bright—

and takes up its real residence in my memory, once night has fallen, and I walk toward the highway, and look at the moving lights in the last of rush hour, and wait to call a car until the traffic thins, daydreaming into nightdreaming, and I sleep, and the underside of my mind looks different when I close my eyes.

Life in motion, or to be more precise, evolving. Reproduction, not mere repetition.

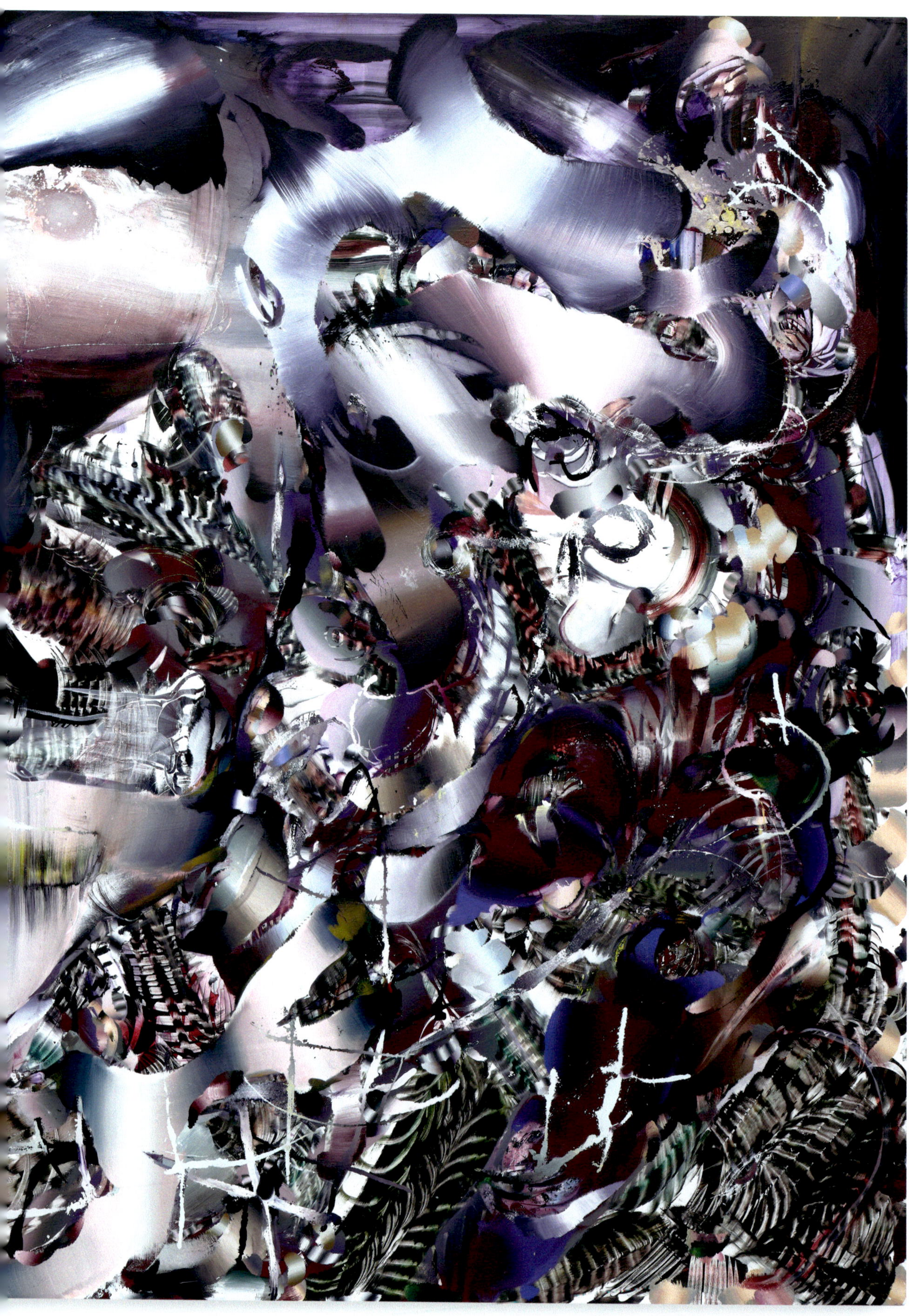

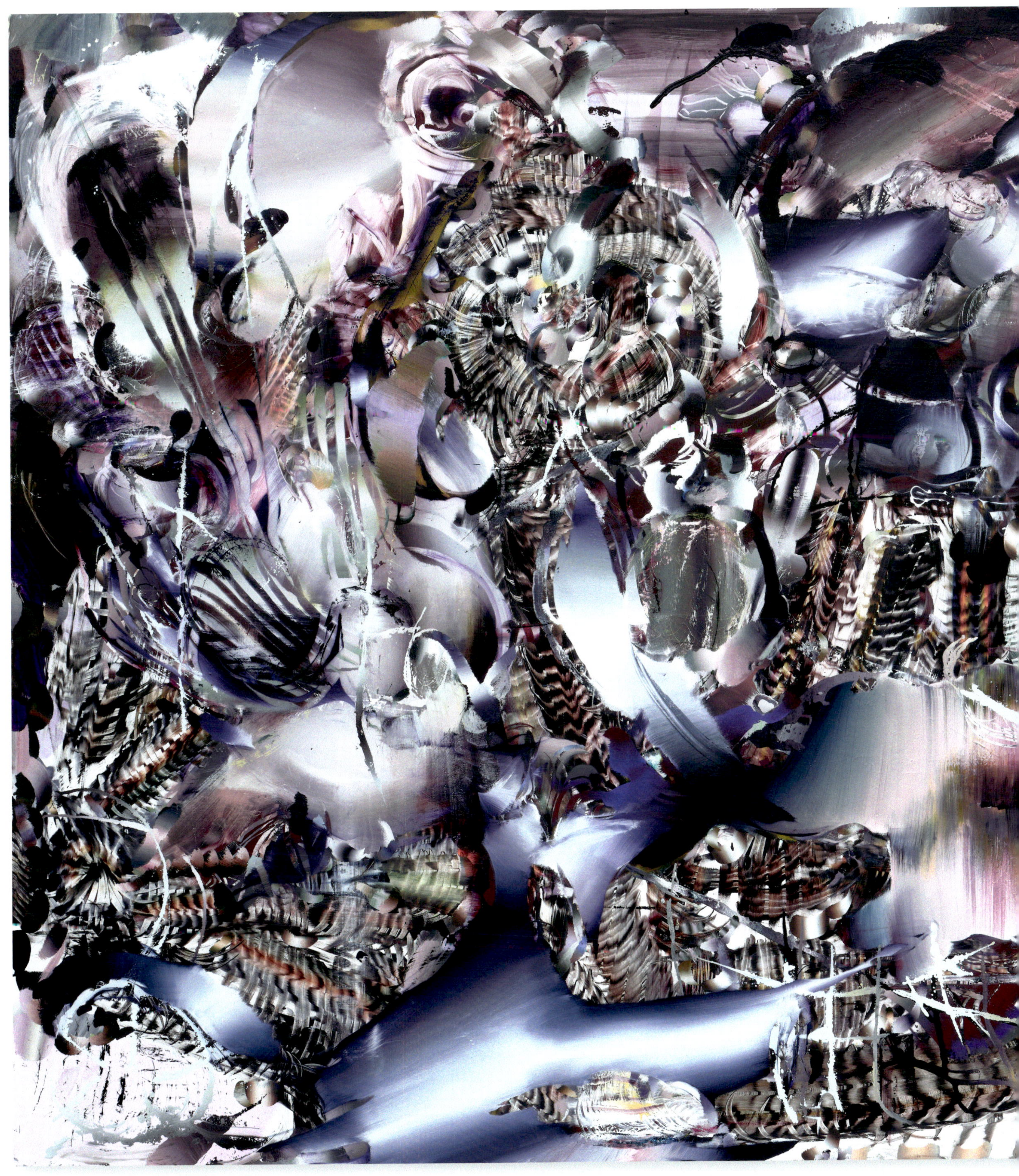

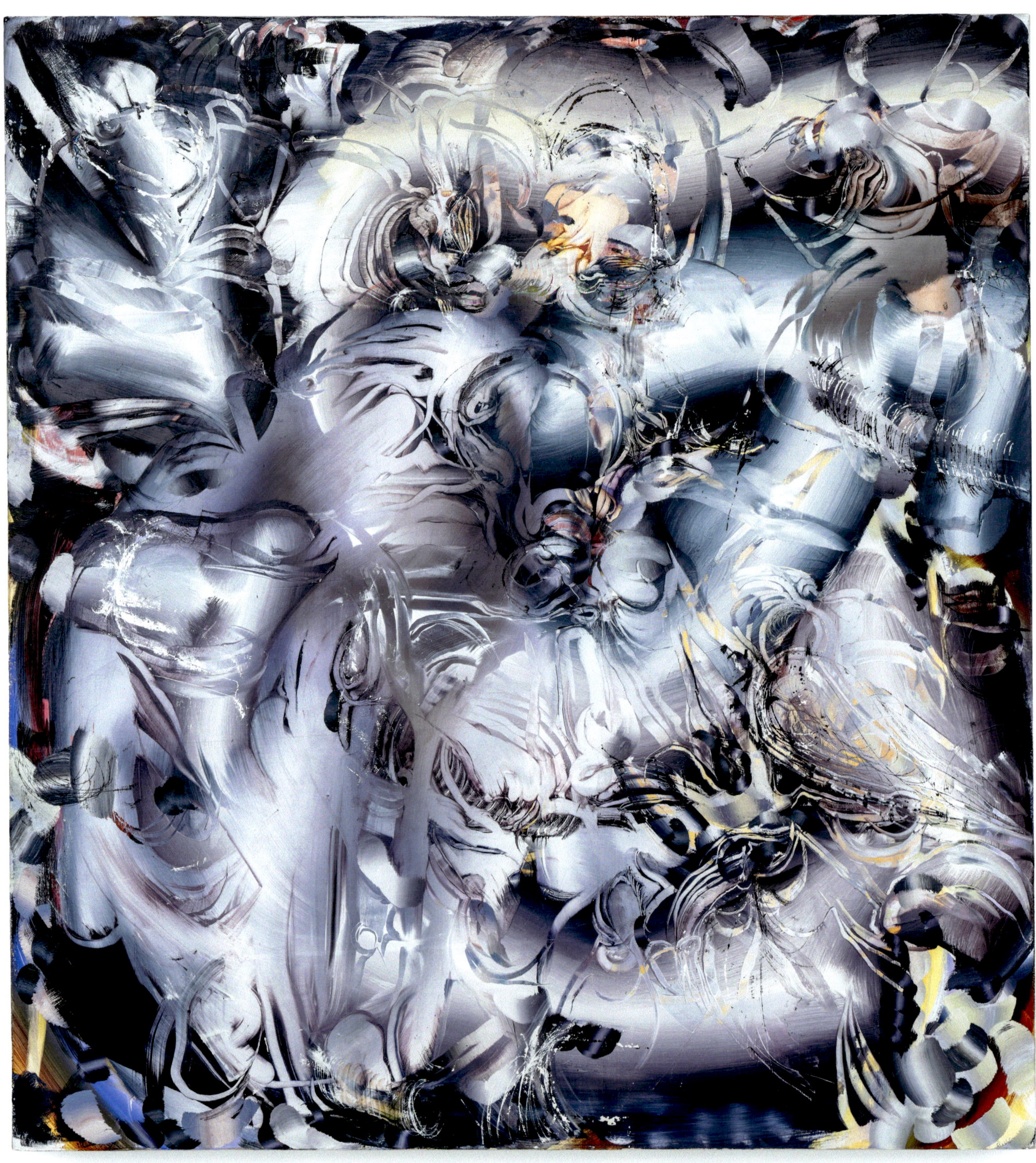

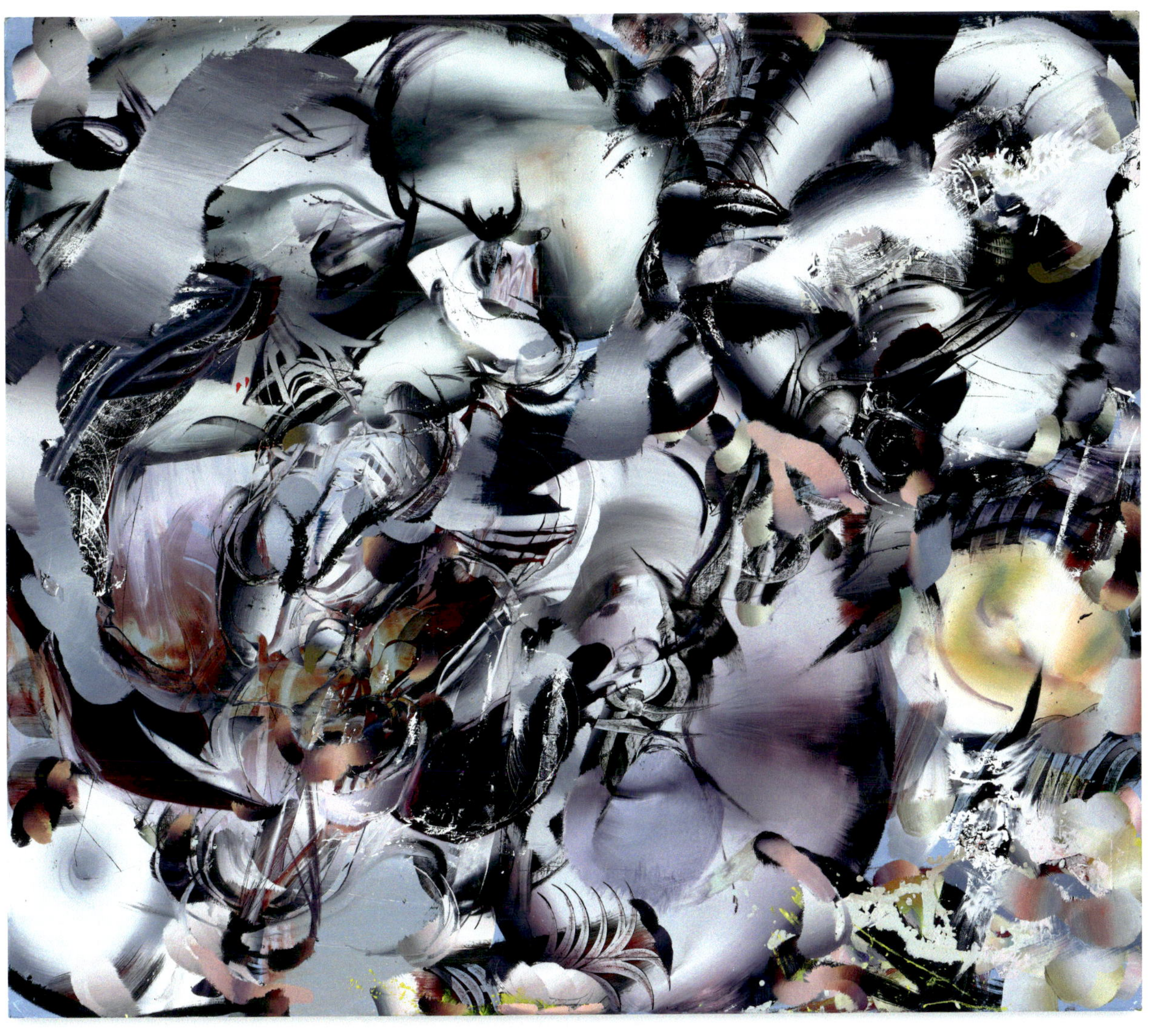

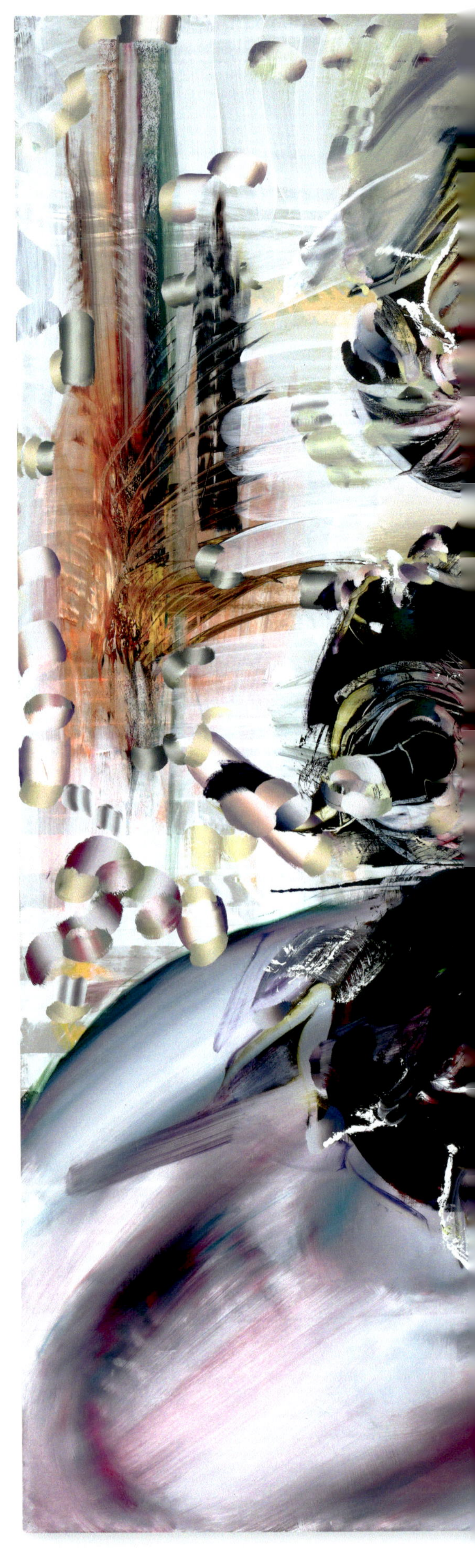

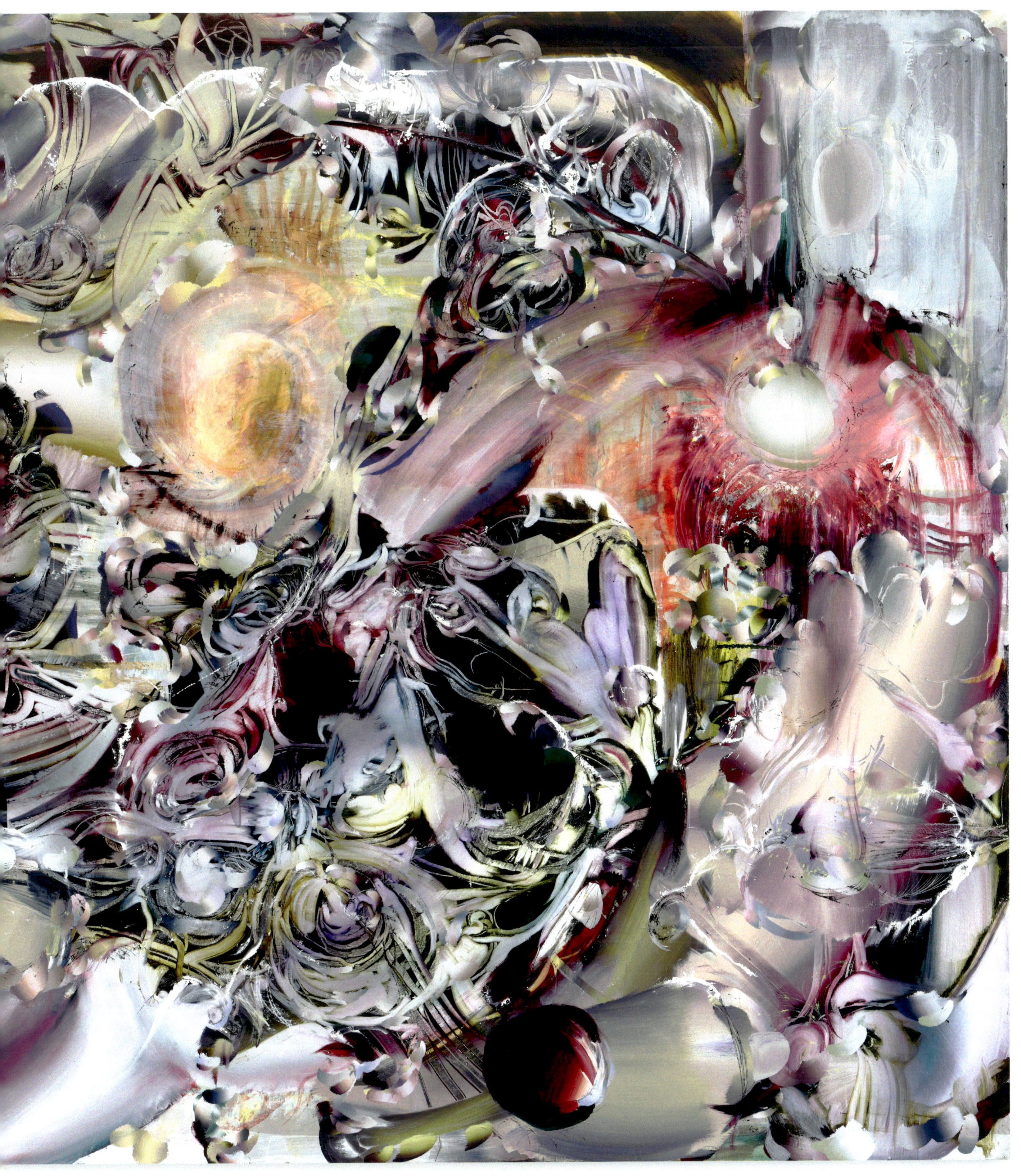

"When I discover something, I have to be able to reproduce it to earn it," Lauren said, "but nothing is *repeatable*. When a discovery becomes repeatable, I have to move on."

Reproduction, not repetition. Gesture and movement giving birth, motion engendering new motion.

"I like the moiré effect that happens to my paintings on a screen," said Lauren, but we established—she established *scientifically*—that the paintings can't be miniaturized. Their mechanical reproduction makes a kind of textile toward which one can have a friendly feeling.

I'm sure my eye is jaundiced, fatigued, and probably dulled by my screens and what is repeated on them, by how accustomed they have become, at this point, to too seldom sweeping over distances. It's the omnipresent cliché that must be acknowledged.

But in being beguiled, the senses can reawaken.

From the suctioning effect on my eyeballs to the proportions of the painter's arm and body rhyming in the sweep that finds my eye, what I see's a phenomenon of solitude that is protected and preserved by the sense that it, too, has secrets.

A portion of what I see is protecting something from me, and I respect it for doing so.

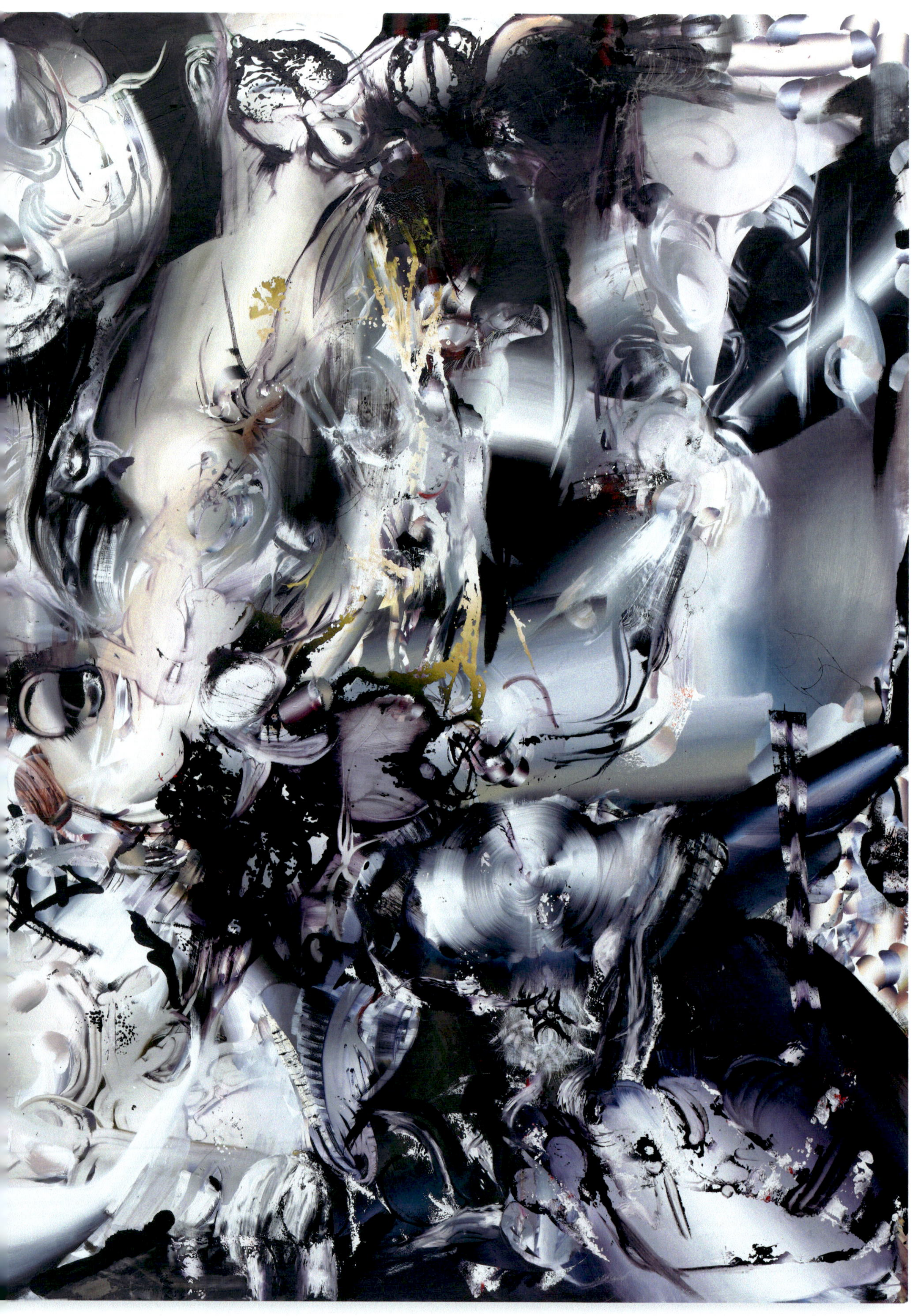

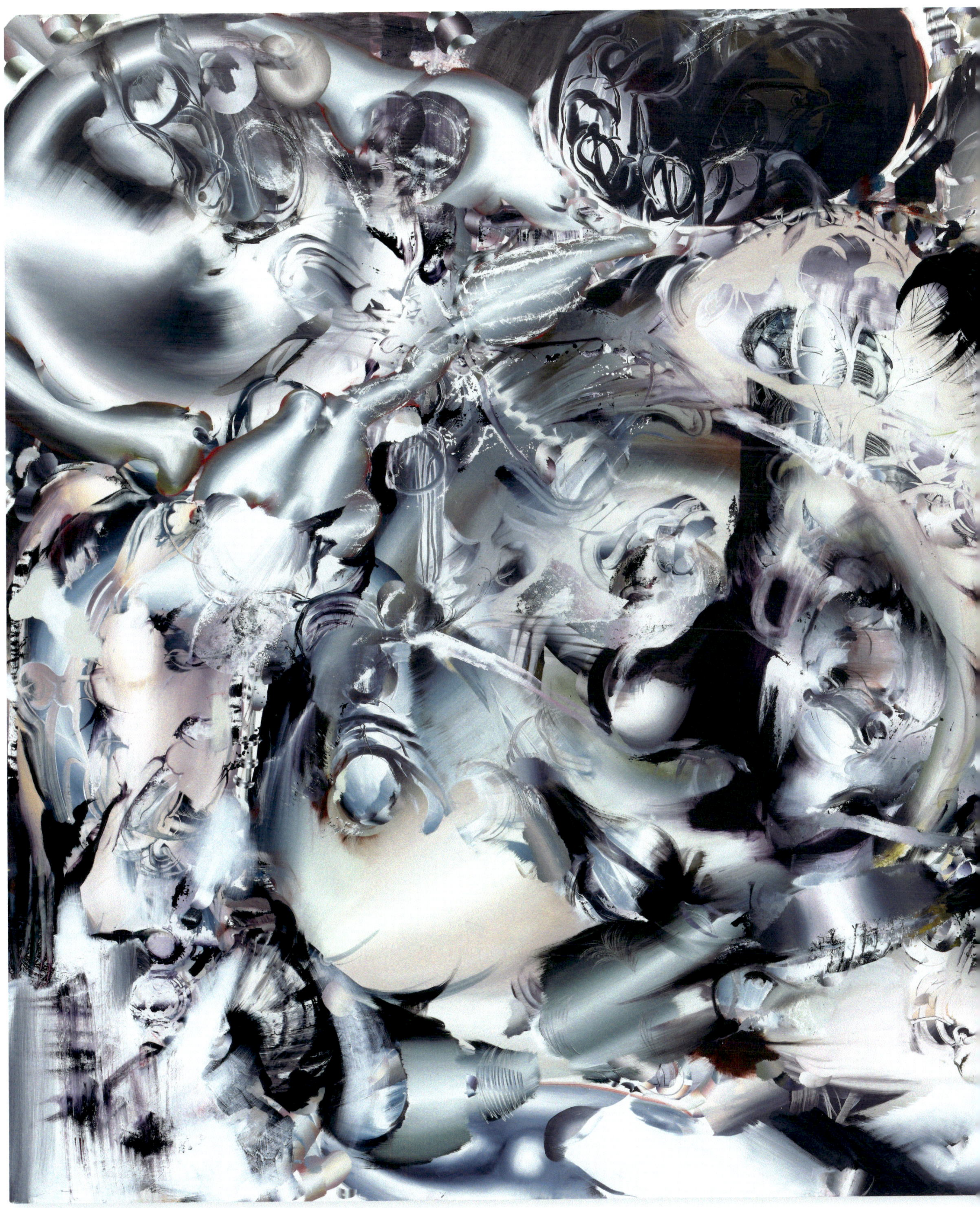

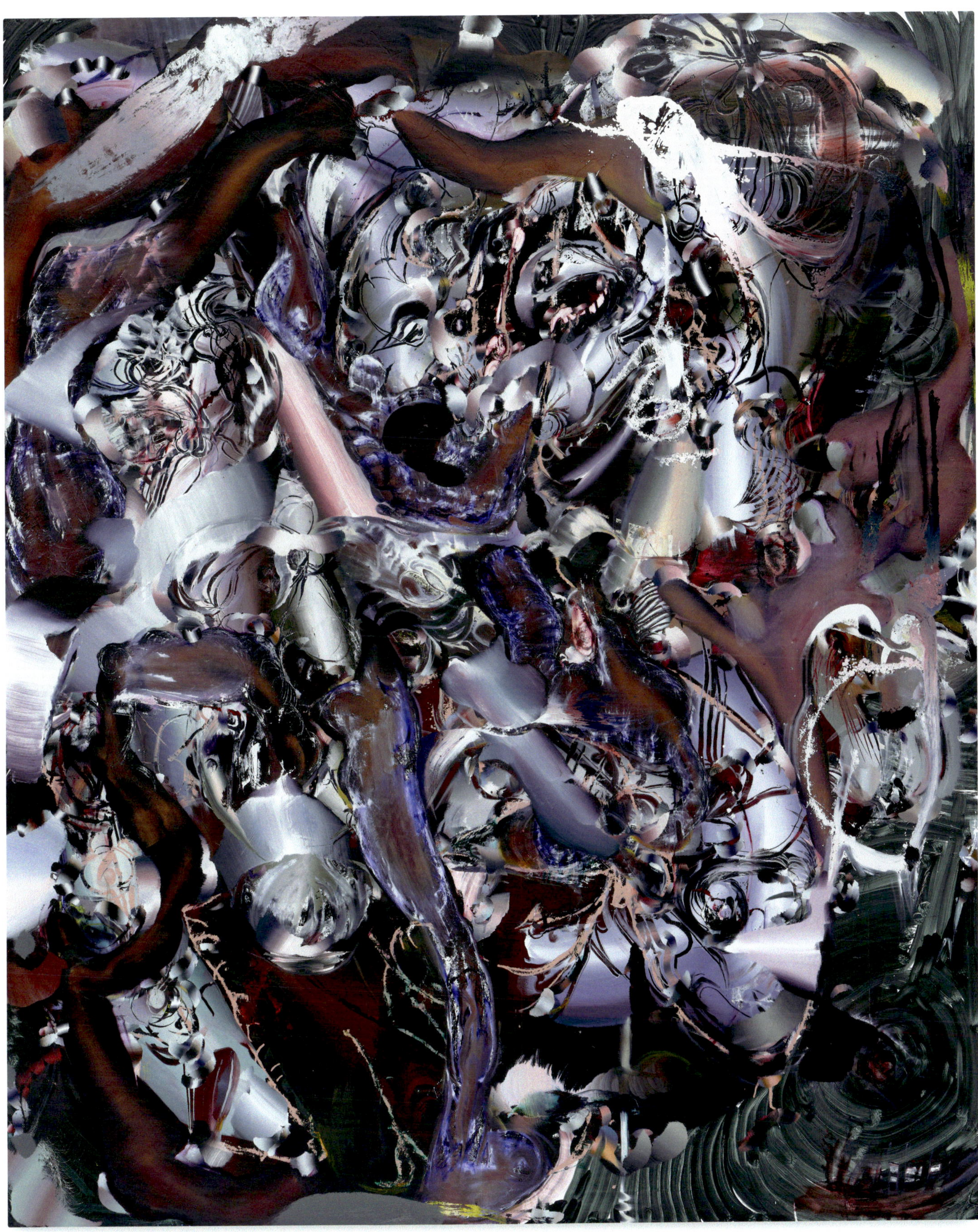

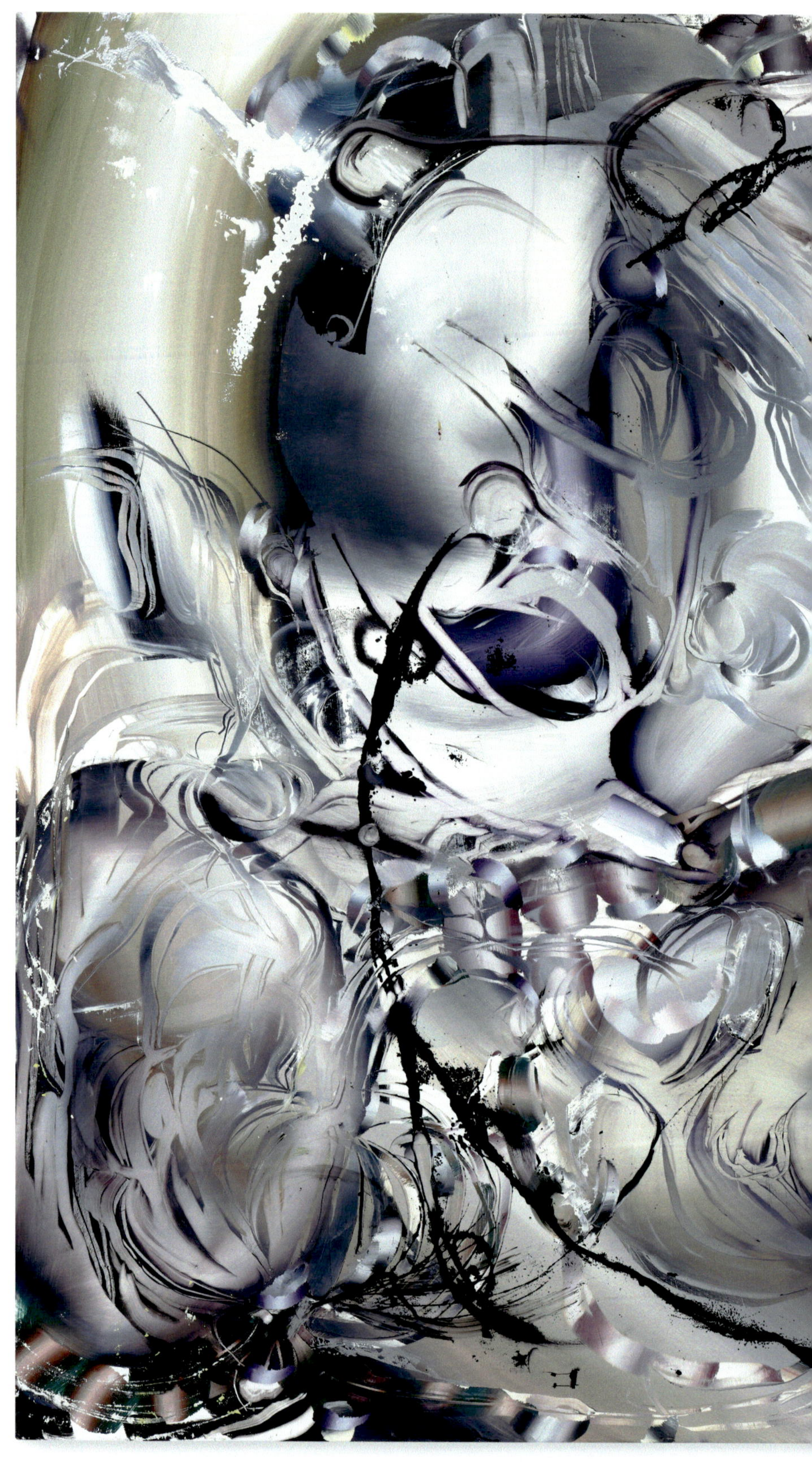

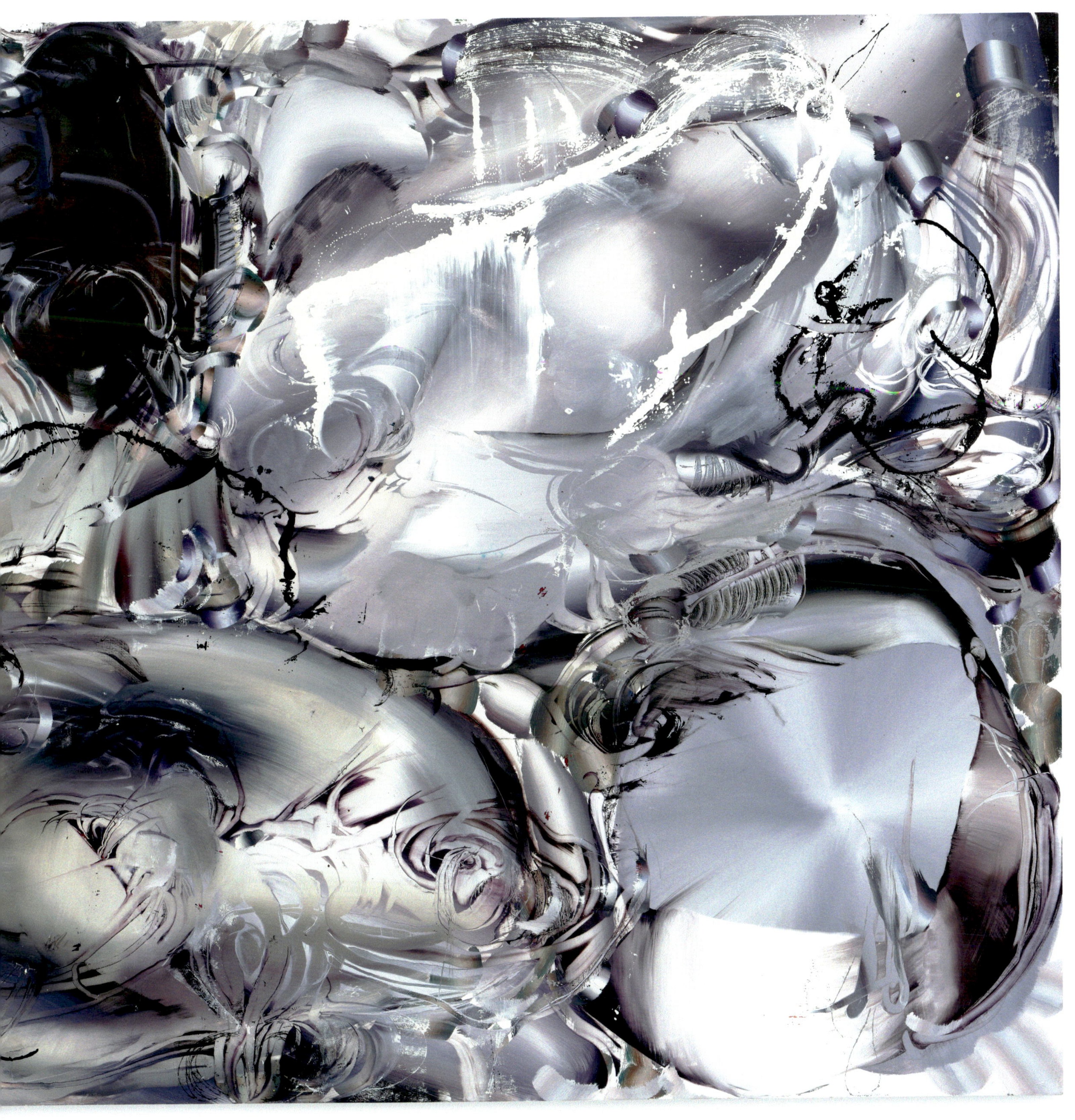

insects in my eyes
light's little waving legs

a millipede of light
a whole millennium

eggs, ears
& egg ears

fertilized albumen, whites
of the eye, ancient egg

tempera, furred
grey belly of the bat

at dusk
grazing the top of the water

hunting for dinner

– AR

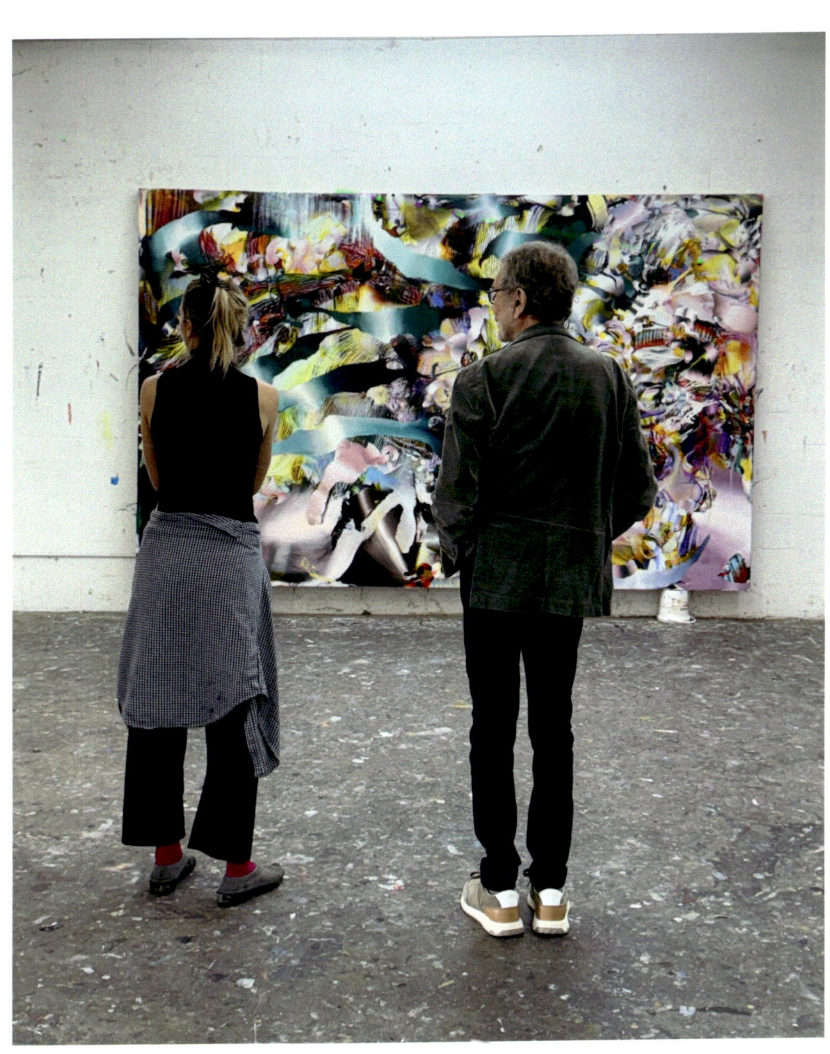

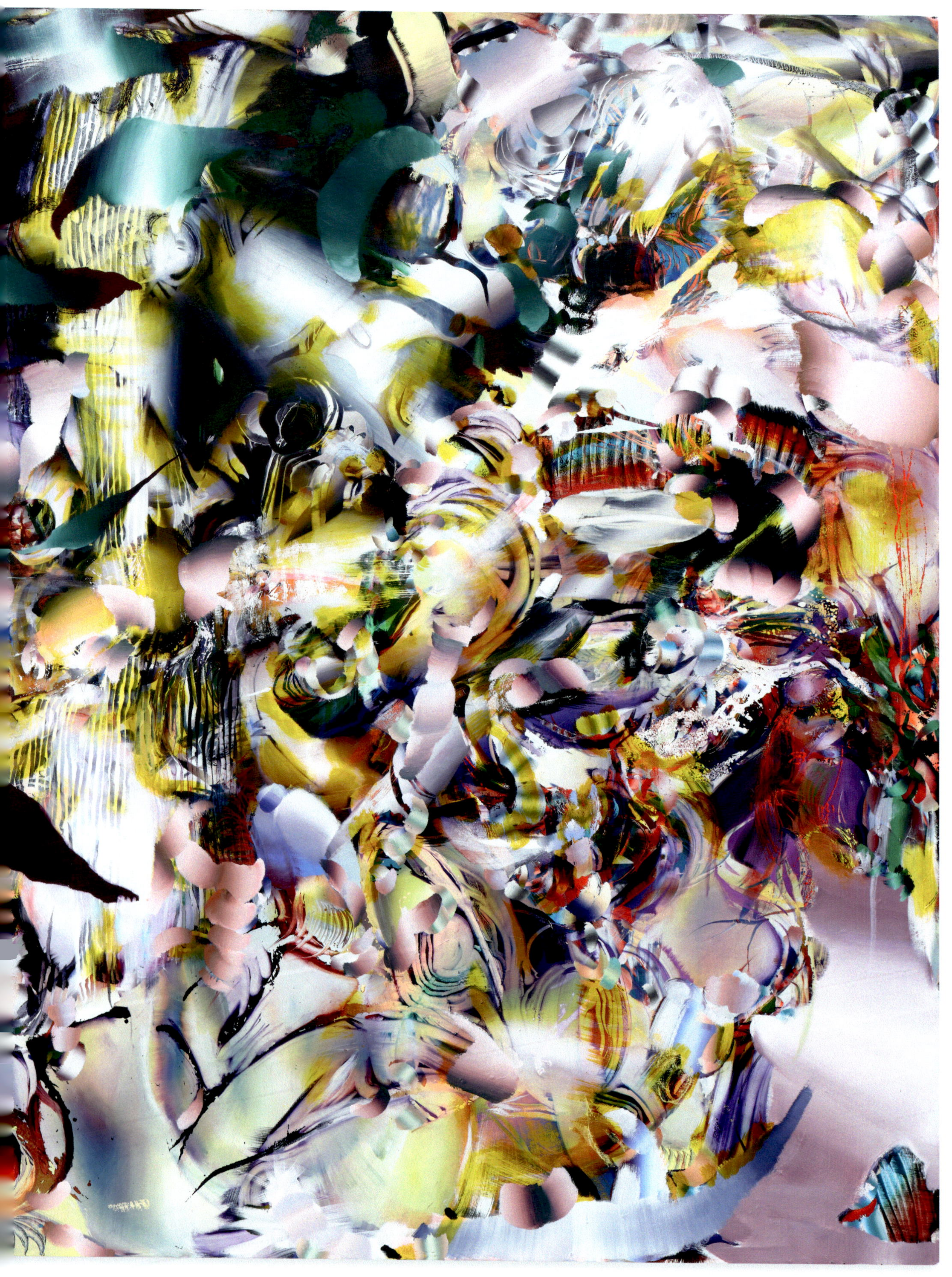

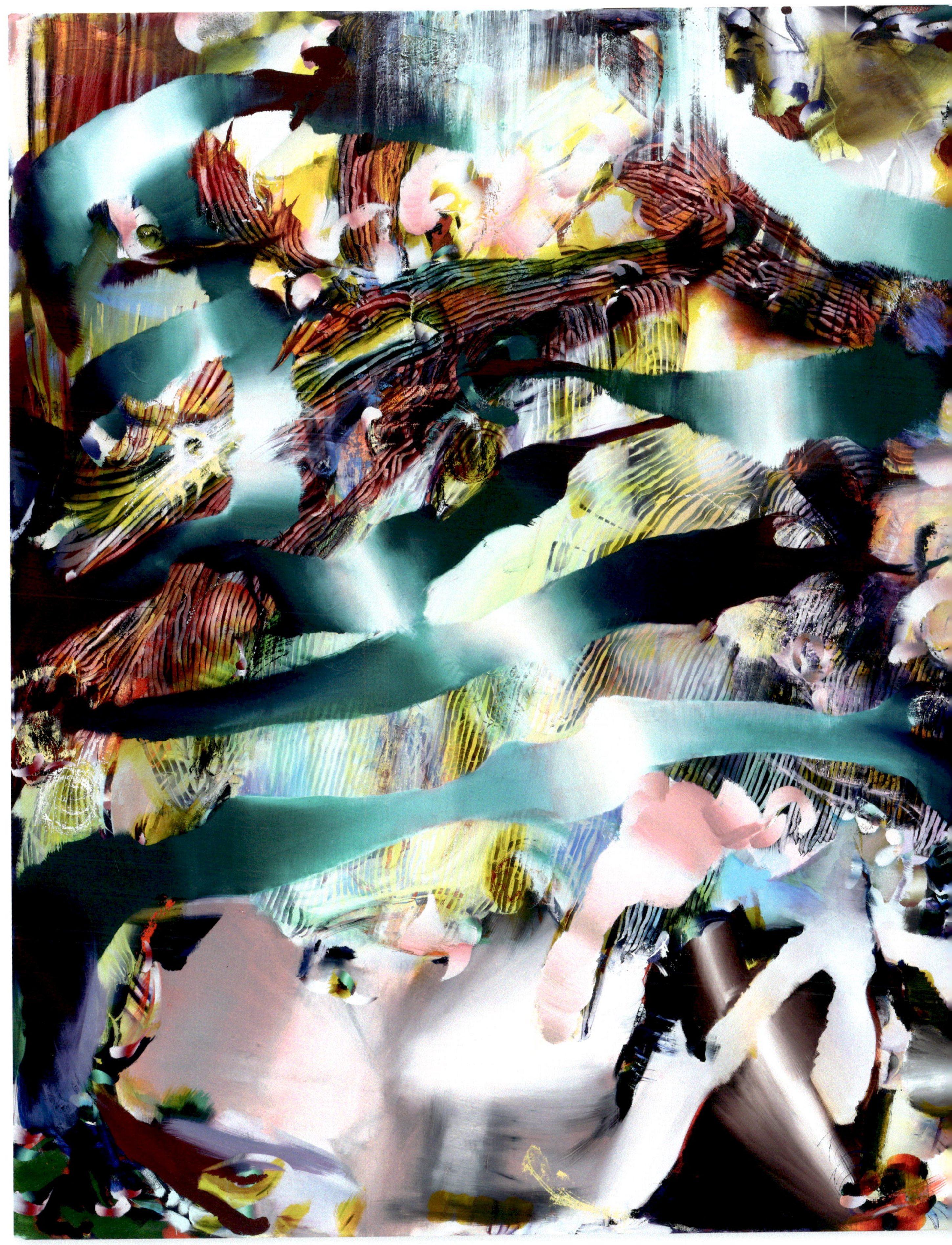

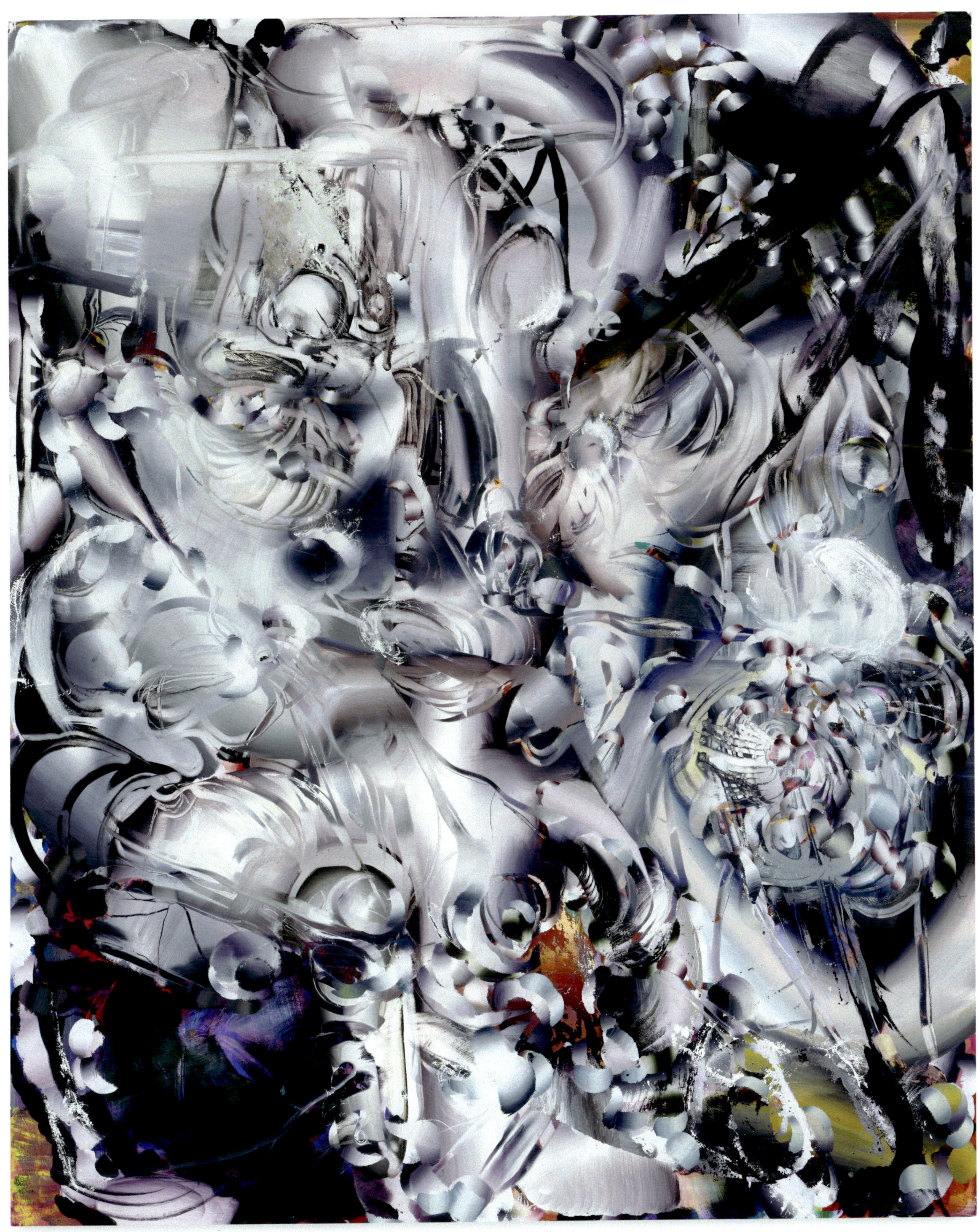

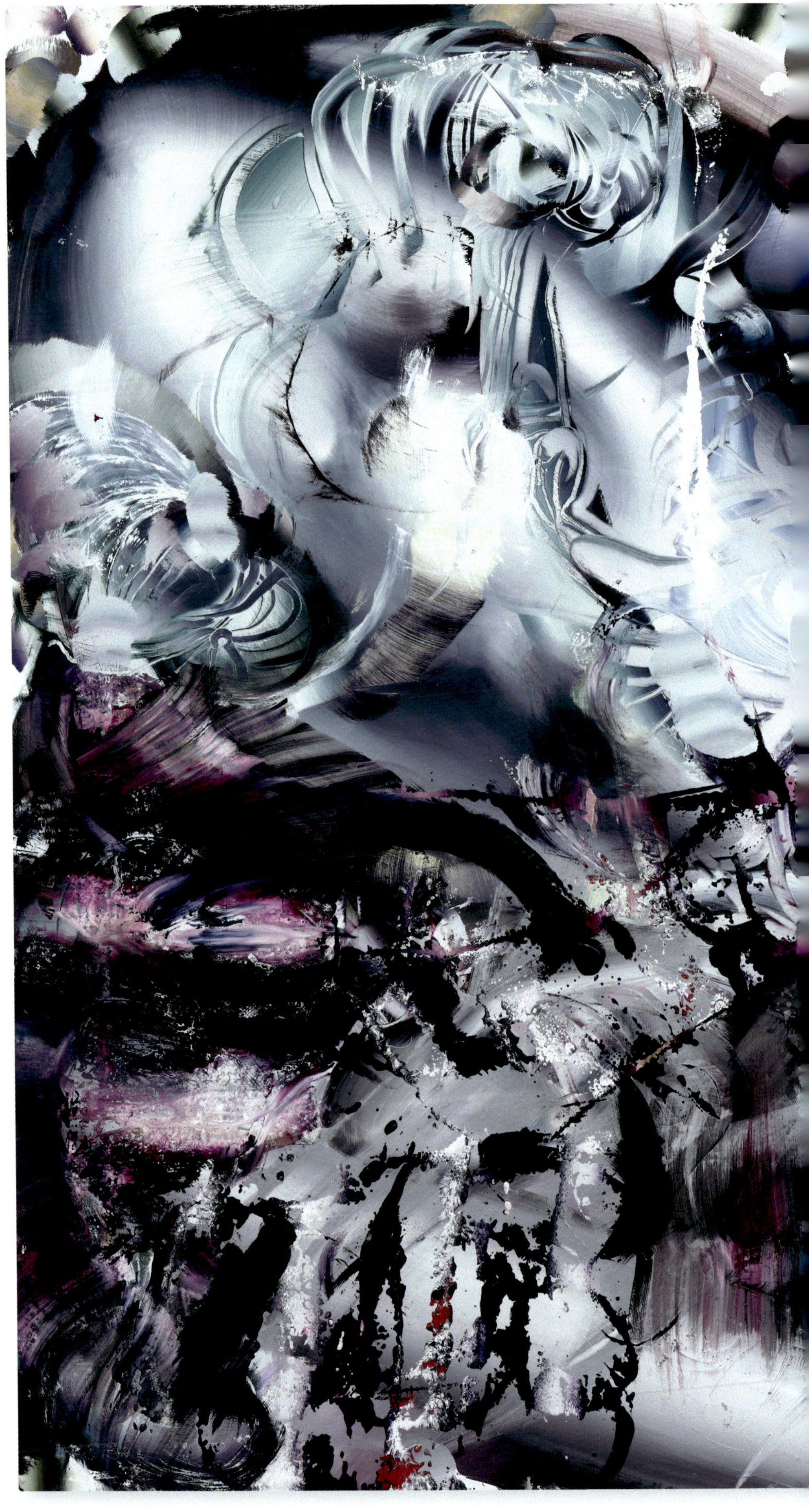

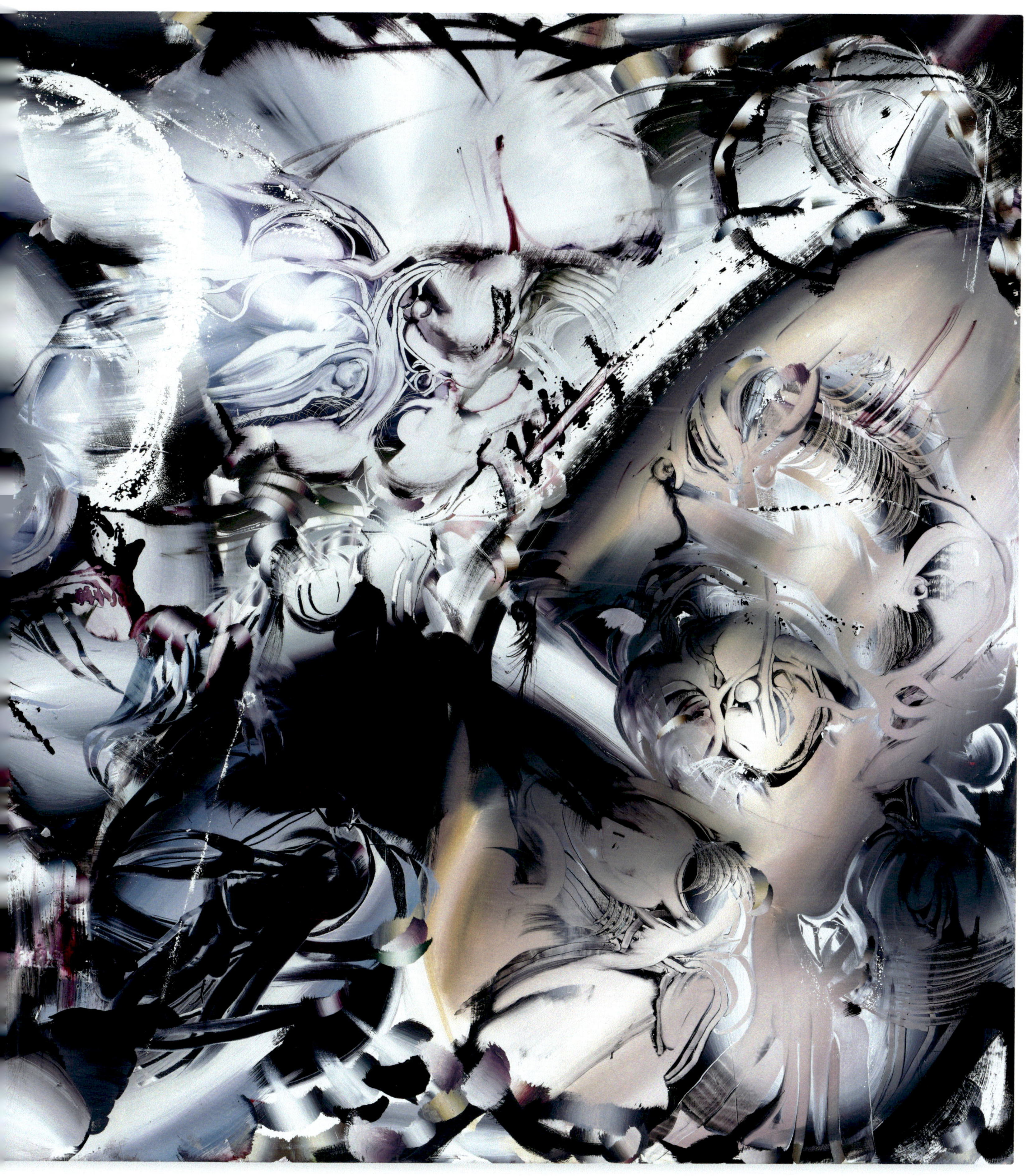

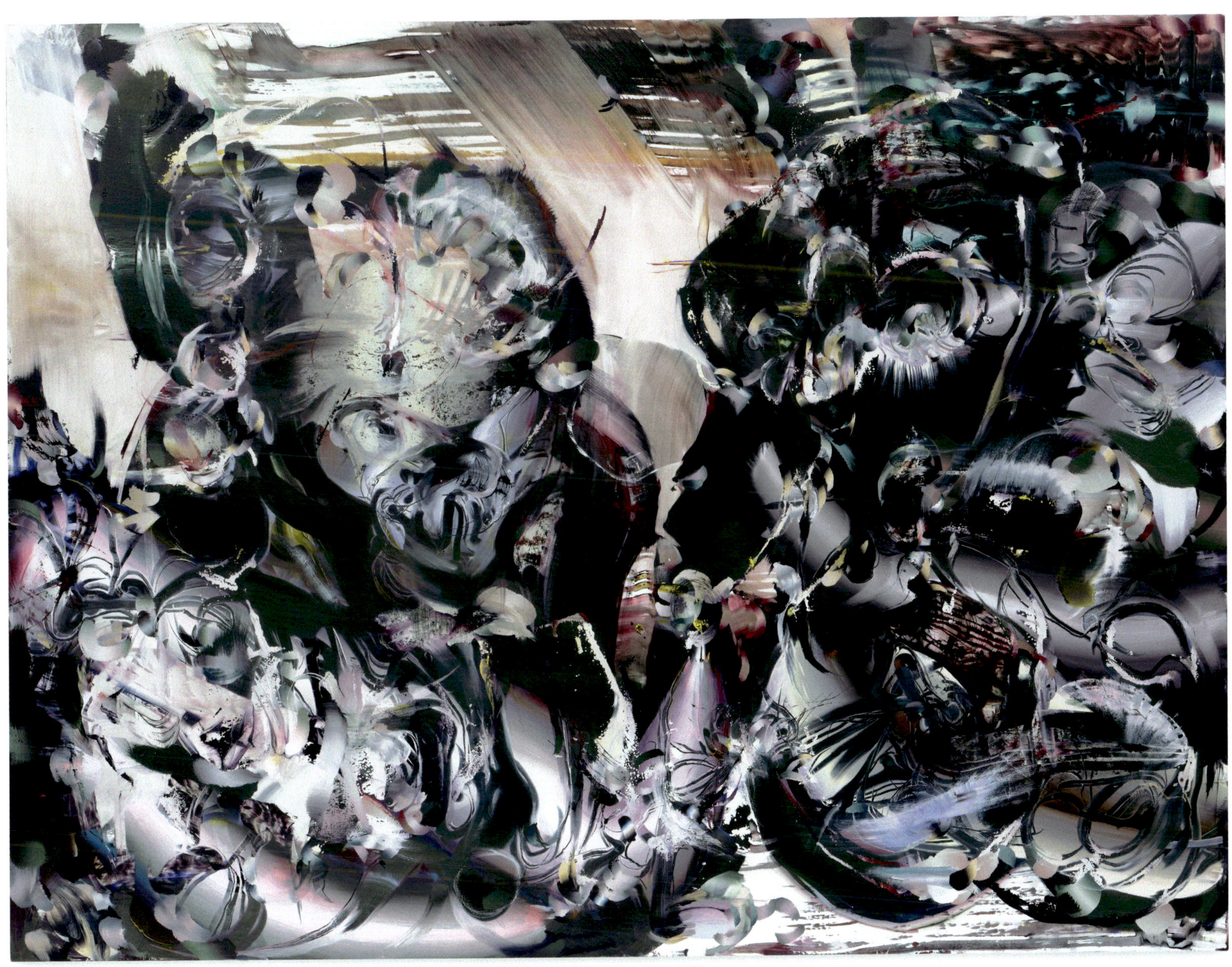

CHUTES

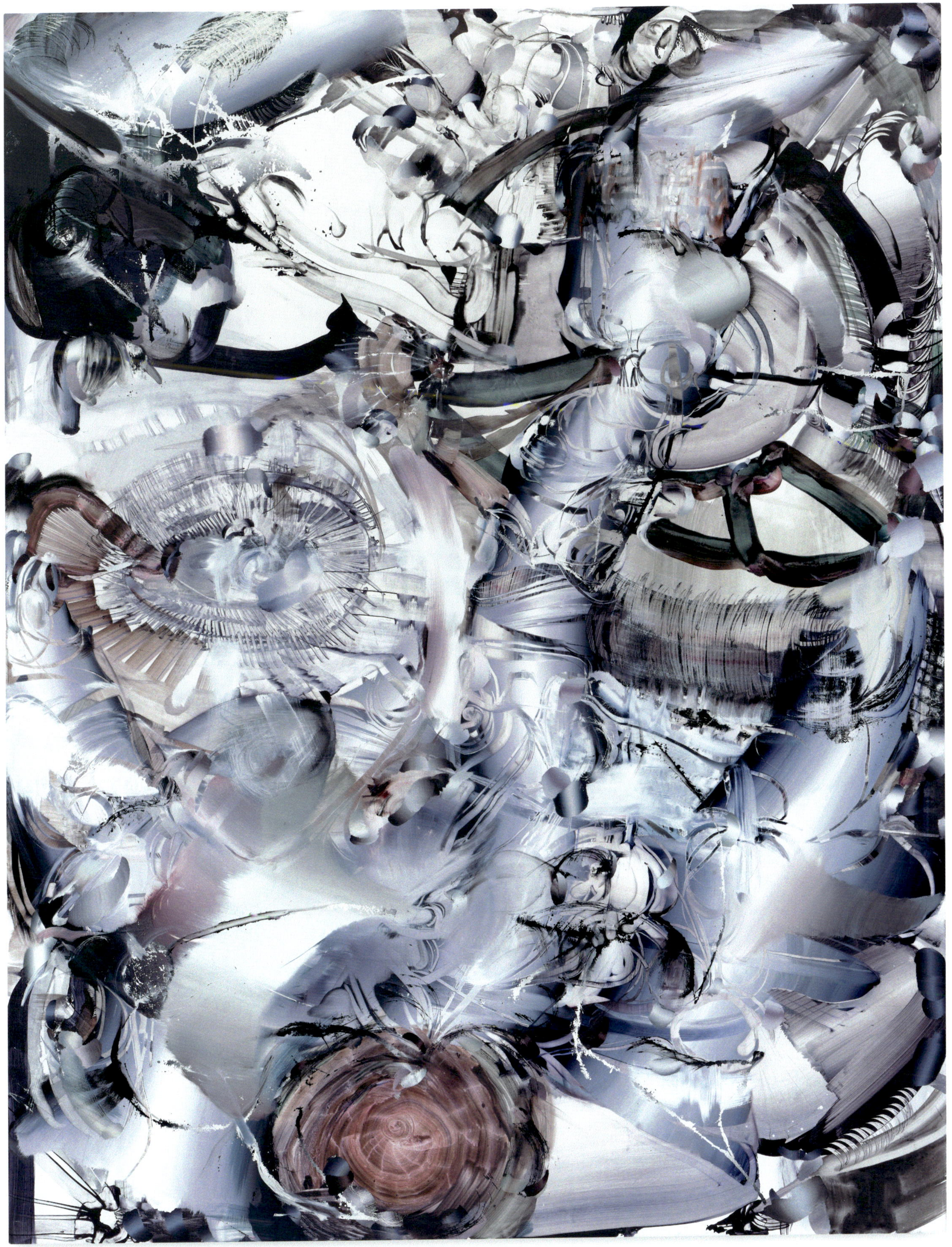

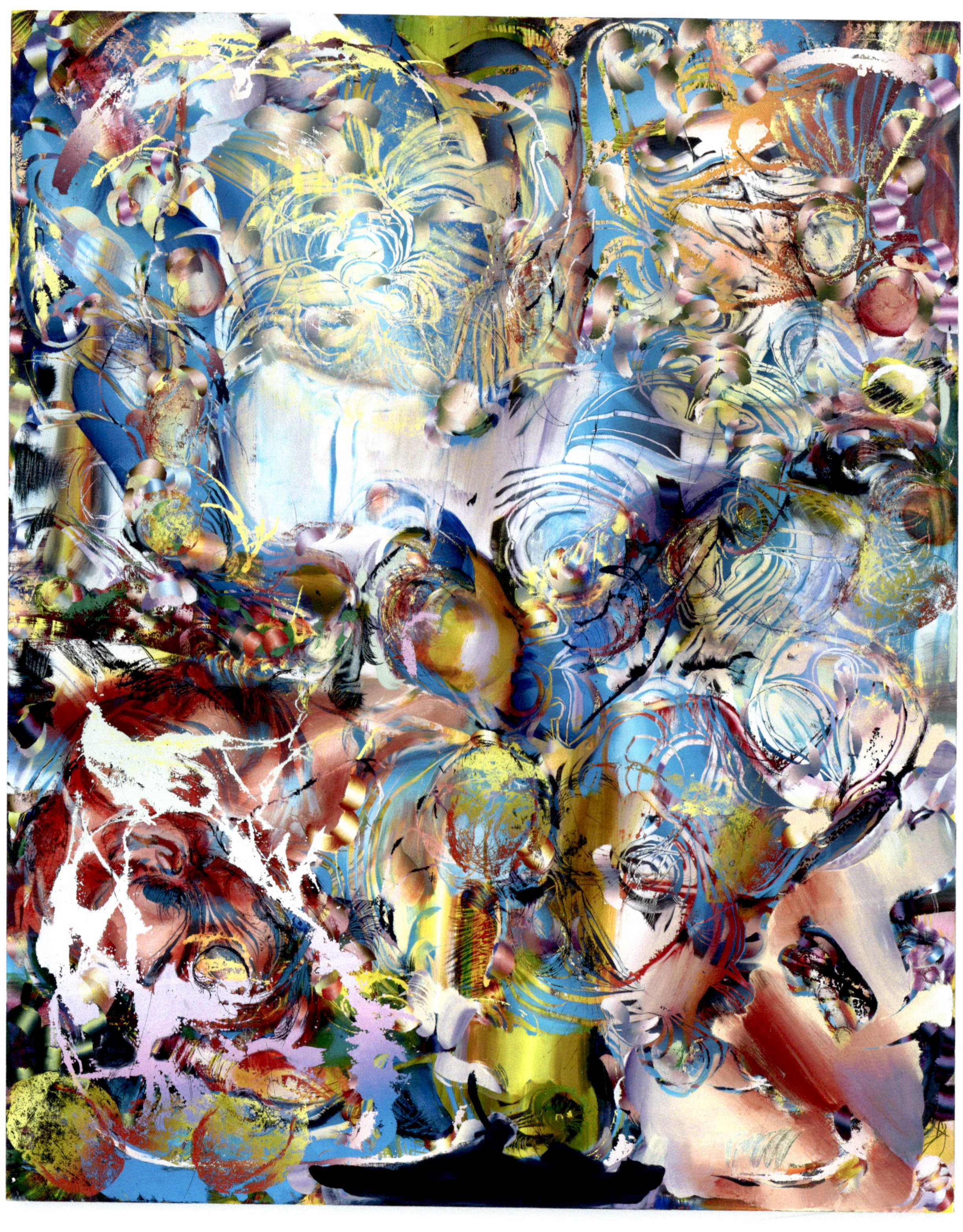

LIST OF WORKS

THE COLD VEIN | 2025
oil on canvas
78 × 156"
pp. 6–7

COLT | 2025
oil on canvas
82 × 72"
p. 9

PITCH | 2025
oil on canvas
72 × 120"
p. 11

GRISTLE | 2025
oil on canvas
54 × 50"
p. 12

GRIS | 2026
oil on canvas
36 ½ × 42"
p. 13

EYELETS OF ALKALINE | 2025
oil on canvas
78 ¾ × 98 ½"
pp. 14–15

GRIZELJ | 2025
oil on canvas
90 × 144"
p. 17

UNBECOMING | 2025
oil on canvas
86 × 71"
p. 19

GLISSADE | 2025
oil on canvas
55 × 90 ½"
pp. 20–21

THE SILK OF RELEASE | 2025
oil on canvas
90 × 144"
p. 23

FALL LINE | 2025
oil on canvas
86 × 71"
p. 25

KRUMMHOLZ | 2025
oil on canvas
48 ¼ × 72 ½"
pp. 26–27

RIME | 2025
oil on canvas
60 × 80"
p. 29

CHUTES | 2025
oil on canvas
92 × 72"
p. 31

LOWING | 2024
oil on canvas
86 × 71"
p. 32

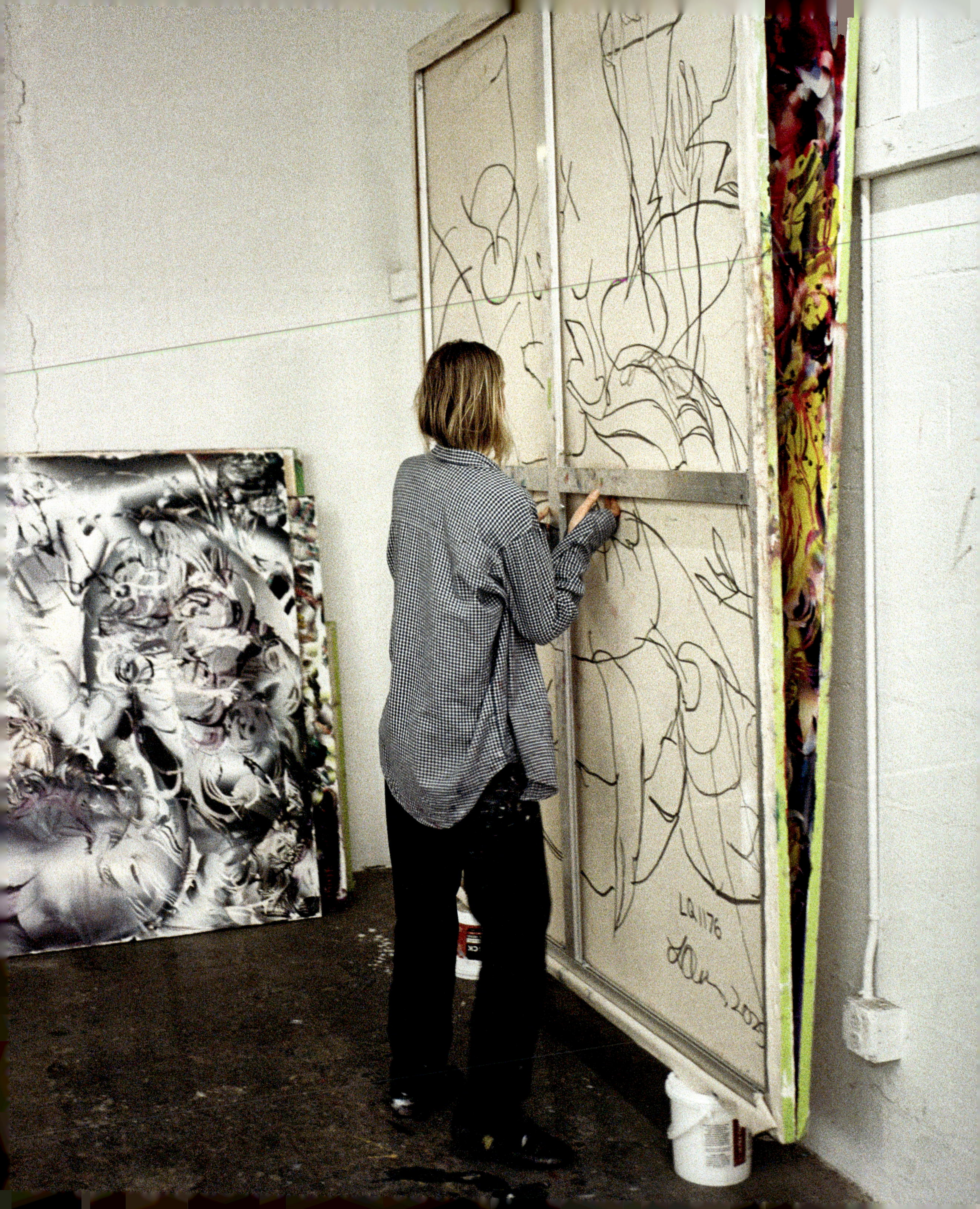
LQ1176

PUBLIC COLLECTIONS

Columbus Museum of Art, Ohio

Dallas Museum of Art, Texas

FAMM - Female Artists of the Mougins Museum, Mougins, Provence, France

Fine Arts Museums of San Francisco

Fundación Medianoche, Granada, Spain

High Museum of Art, Atlanta, Georgia

Hirshhorn Museum and Sculpture Garden, Smithsonian Institution, Washington, D.C.

Institute of Contemporary Art, Miami

Kistefos Museum, Jevnaker, Norway

Long Museum, Shanghai

Museum of Contemporary Art, Los Angeles

Museum of Fine Arts, Boston

Nerman Museum of Contemporary Art, Johnson County Community College, Overland Park, Kansas

Pérez Art Museum, Miami

Phoenix Art Museum, Arizona

The Smart Museum of Art at the University of Chicago

Walker Art Center, Minneapolis, Minnesota

Yuz Museum, Shanghai

ACKNOWLEDGMENTS

I would like to extend my heartfelt gratitude to Arne Glimcher for your unwavering belief in my work, your extraordinary generosity, clarity, and tenacity. Your friendship and mentorship have been a guiding principle in the studio.

Thank you to Marc Glimcher for your continued support, enthusiasm, and problem-solving. To Talia Rosen for all your endeavors behind the scenes. To Oliver Shultz for your brilliance and presence in the studio, and for always keeping the context of the work in focus.

I am grateful to Ariana Reines for converting the ineffable into lyric and for meeting the work with such precision and openness. And to everyone who has had a hand in bringing this book and show to fruition, including Gillian Canavan, Genevieve Day, Josh Friedman, Colleen Grennan, Tomo Makiura, Paul Pollard, Samanthe Rubell, Dylan Siegel, John Zinonos, and the entire Pace apparatus.

Thank you to Steven Taylor for having the premonition to photograph the studio at a critical moment, and to Marten Elder and Josh White for their photography and relentless color editing. To Trevor Jones for your calming presence and assistance over a cruel summer. To my friend Steve Aldahl for lending me his mother's name, Grizelj, as well as several other crucial painting titles. To all my LA artist friends who visited the studio and saw this work take shape over the past year and a half.

And to my sweetheart, Anthony Salvador, for your support on all fronts.

—Lauren Quin

Lauren Quin is an LA artist. It is therefore an automatic honor to present her exhibition at Pace's gallery in Los Angeles. From my first visit to Lauren's studio in the late days of the pandemic, I have drawn energy from her restless quest for new possibilities in painting. Our show together at 125 Newbury in 2024—her debut in New York City—was a joy. I have been privileged to observe the development of her practice since then. It has been nothing short of thrilling.

Many individuals contributed to the realization of this extraordinary exhibition and to the making of this book, which is both a documentation and an extension of the show.

I would like to thank Anthony Salvador, whose love for Lauren and commitment to her work reminds me of the indelible link between creativity and care. That same care is reflected in the writing of Ariana Reines, who has penned a moving and provocative text on Lauren's work. I am deeply indebted to Paul Pollard and Tomo Makiura for their work designing and producing this book, and to the entire Publications team in New York, led by Gillian Canavan.

My gratitude goes to Bill Griffin for his leadership, to Joshua Friedman for his engagement, and to Genevieve Day, Colleen Grennan, and Meghan Coleman for their enthusiasm. Indeed, I am indebted to the full team in LA. I also thank Amelia Redgrift, Samanthe Rubell, and my son Marc.

On my own team, I am grateful to Talia Rosen for steadfastly serving as Lauren's daily support, as well as to Dylan Siegel, who has been instrumental to the publication and the organization of the show. Oliver Shultz has been an interlocutor and thought partner, accompanying me intellectually and literally on my many visits to Lauren's studio. Our conversations about the power of her work remain vital and ongoing.

My gratitude goes most of all to Lauren herself. She has once again astonished me, with paintings that expand the possibilities of our perception, bringing the grammar of abstraction to unforeseen trajectories. The works are both a challenge and an invitation and I am grateful to everyone who contributed to bringing them to the public's awareness.

—Arne Glimcher

Published on the occasion of
Lauren Quin
Eyelets of Alkaline
January 31 – March 28, 2026

Pace Gallery
1201 South La Brea Avenue
Los Angeles

p. 4: *Chutes*, 2025 (detail)

Photography:
Martin Alder: pp. 4, 6–7, 9, 11, 13, 14–15, 17, 19, 20–21, 23, 25, 26–27, 29, 31
Oliver Shultz: p. 24
Steven Taylor: pp. 2–3, 34
Josh White: pp. 12, 32

Creative Director: Tomo Makiura
Production: Paul Pollard
Editor in Chief: Gillian Canavan
Editorial Manager: Madeline Gilmore
Rights & Reproductions: Vincent Wilcke
Color Separations and Printing:
Meridian Printing, a GHP Media company, East Greenwich, RI

Typeset in Roxborough and Apolline

ISBN: 978-1-948701-34-1
Library of Congress Control Number: 2026931321

Available through ARTBOOK | D.A.P.
75 Broad Street, Suite 630 New York, NY 10004
www.artbook.com